U·X·L

American Decades

1950·1959

U·X·L American Decades
1950·1959

Tom Pendergast
& Sara Pendergast,
Editors

Detroit • New York • San Diego • San Francisco • Cleveland • New Haven, Conn. • Waterville, Maine • London • Munich

THOMSON

GALE

U•X•L American Decades, 1950–1959

Tom Pendergast and Sara Pendergast, Editors

Project Editors
Diane Sawinski, Julie L. Carnagie, and Christine Slovey

Editorial
Elizabeth Anderson

Permissions
Shalice Shah-Caldwell

Imaging and Multimedia
Dean Dauphinais

Product Design
Pamela A.E. Galbreath

Composition
Evi Seoud

Manufacturing
Rita Wimberley

For permission to use material from this product, submit your request via Web at http://www.gale-edit.com/permissions, or you may download our Permissions Request form and submit your request by fax or mail to:

Permissions Department
The Gale Group, Inc.
27500 Drake Rd.
Farmington Hills, MI 48331-3535
Permissions Hotline:
248-699-8006 or 800-877-4253, ext. 8006
Fax: 248-699-8074 or 800-762-4058

Cover photograph reproduced courtesy of The Library of Congress.

While every effort has been made to ensure the reliability of the information presented in this publication, The Gale Group, Inc. does not guarantee the accuracy of the data contained herein. The Gale Group, Inc. accepts no payment for listing; and inclusion in the publication of any organization, agency, institution, publication, service, or individual does not imply endorsement of the editors or publisher. Errors brought to the attention of the publisher and verified to the satisfaction of the publisher will be corrected in future editions.

Vol. 1: 0-7876-6455-3
Vol. 2: 0-7876-6456-1
Vol. 3: 0-7876-6457-X
Vol. 4: 0-7876-6458-8
Vol. 5: 0-7876-6459-6
Vol. 6: 0-7876-6460-X
Vol. 7: 0-7876-6461-8
Vol. 8: 0-7876-6462-6
Vol. 9: 0-7876-6463-4
Vol. 10: 0-7876-6464-2

LIBRARY OF CONGRESS CATALOGING-IN-PUBLICATION DATA

U•X•L American decades
    p. cm.
Includes bibliographical references and index.
    Contents: v. 1. 1900-1910—v. 2. 1910-1919—v. 3.1920-1929—v. 4. 1930-1939—v. 5.
    1940-1949—v. 6. 1950-1959—v. 7. 1960-1969—v. 8. 1970-1979—v. 9.1980-1989—v. 10.
    1990-1999.
    Summary: A ten-volume overview of the twentieth century which explores such topics
    as the arts, economy, education, government, politics, fashions, health, science, tech-
    nology, and sports which characterize each decade.
    ISBN 0-7876-6454-5 (set: hardcover: alk. paper)
    1. United States—Civilization—20th century—Juvenile literature. 2. United States—
    History—20th century—Juvenile literature. [1. United States—Civilization—20th cen-
    tury. 2. United States—History—20th century.] I. UXL (Firm) II. Title: UXL American
    decades. III. Title: American decades.
E169.1.U88 2003
973.91—dc21
                                                            2002010176

Printed in the United States of America
10 9 8 7 6 5 4 3

Contents

Reader's Guide

U•X•L American Decades provides a broad overview of the major events and people that helped to shape American society throughout the twentieth century. Each volume in this ten-volume set chronicles a single decade and begins with an introduction to that decade and a timeline of major events in twentieth-century America. Following are eight chapters devoted to these categories of American endeavor:

• Arts and Entertainment

• Business and the Economy

• Education

• Government, Politics, and Law

• Lifestyles and Social Trends

• Medicine and Health

• Science and Technology

• Sports

These chapters are then divided into five sections:

Chronology: A timeline of significant events within the chapter's particular field.

Overview: A summary of the events and people detailed in that chapter.

Headline Makers: Short biographical accounts of key people and their achievements during the decade.

❖ **Topics in the News:** A series of short topical essays describing events and people within the chapter's theme.

✛ **For More Information:** A section that lists books and Web sites directing the student to further information about the events and people covered in the chapter.

OTHER FEATURES

Each volume of *U•X•L American Decades* contains more than eighty black-and-white photographs and illustrations that bring the events and people discussed to life and sidebar boxes that expand on items of high interest to readers. Concluding each volume is a general bibliography of books and Web sites that explore the particular decade in general and a thorough subject index that allows readers to easily locate the events, people, and places discussed throughout that volume of *U•X•L American Decades*.

COMMENTS AND SUGGESTIONS

We welcome your comments on *U•X•L American Decades* and suggestions for other history topics to consider. Please write: Editors, *U•X•L American Decades*, U•X•L, 27500 Drake Rd., Farmington Hills, MI 48331-3535; call toll-free: 1-800-877-4253; fax: 248-699-8097; or send e-mail via http://www.galegroup.com.

Chronology of the 1950s

1950: The hepatitis A virus is isolated and photographed.

1950: Blood tests for tuberculosis are introduced.

1950: **January 19–22** The Ladies' Professional Golf Association (LPGA) holds its inaugural tournament.

1950: **February 9** Wisconsin Senator Joseph McCarthy claims to have a list containing 205 known communists employed in the U.S. State Department.

1950: **March 26** A U.S. Senate investigative committee on organized crime opens its nationwide inquiry.

1950: **April–May** The American Bowling Congress (ABC) ends its white-male-only policy.

1950: **April 18** A patient pronounced dead during surgery is revived through heart massage.

1950: **June 25** North Korean Communist troops cross the 38th parallel into South Korea, resulting in the start of the Korean War.

1950: **August 29** Althea Gibson becomes the first black woman to compete in a national tennis tournament.

1950: **September 19** African American student Heman Marion Sweatt successfully registers at the University of Texas law school, where he had been denied admission four years earlier because of his race.

1950: October 2 *Peanuts*, the comic strip written and drawn by Charles Schulz, debuts in seven U.S. newspapers.

1950: October 16 The New Jersey Supreme Court upholds the practice of reciting five Old Testament verses each day in all public schools.

1950: November 1 Puerto Rican nationalists attempt to assassinate President Harry S Truman.

1951: Chrysler introduces the first production-model car with power steering.

1951: Marion Donovan develops "The Boater," the first disposable diaper.

1951: The nausea-inducing drug antabus is marketed as a cure for alcoholism.

1951: The first full-body X-ray machine is developed.

1951: *The Caine Mutiny,* the war novel by Herman Wouk, is published and soon becomes one of the longest lasting bestsellers of all time.

1951: C. A. Swanson and Sons introduce the first frozen dinners.

1951: February 26 The Twenty-Second Amendment to the Constitution, which limits presidential tenure to two terms, is adopted.

1951: March 2 The National Basketball Association (NBA) holds its first All-Star Game.

1951: April Remington-Rand sells the first commercially available computer, the UNIVAC I.

1951: April 18 New York Yankees rookie Mickey Mantle makes his major league debut.

1951: May 15 AT&T becomes the first American corporation with one million stockholders.

1951: May 25 New York Giants rookie Willie Mays makes his major league debut.

1951: October 10 Joe DiMaggio plays his final game for the New York Yankees.

1952: The McDonald's Golden Arch is designed.

1952: R. Buckminster Fuller displays his geodesic dome concept at New York's Museum of Modern Art.

1952: January *American Bandstand* (1952–89), a popular teen-oriented music program, debuts as a local show in Philadelphia. Dick Clark, its most famous host, comes aboard in 1956.

1952: January 14 *The Today Show* (1952–) debuts on NBC.

1952: January 30 A patient suffering a heart attack is revived by electric shock.

1952: April 29 With the opening of its coeducational College of Arts and Sciences, the University of Rochester terminates its 107-year-old policy of separate men's and women's colleges.

1952: September 19 The first artificial heart valve is put into a human being.

1952: September 23 Rocky Marciano beats Jersey Joe Walcott for the heavyweight championship.

1952: November *Bwana Devil*, the first 3-D movie, is released.

1952: November 12 An all-white North Carolina jury convicts a black man of assault for "leering" at a white woman 27 feet away.

1952: November 13 An artificial pacemaker is used to regulate heart rhythm.

1953: The Raytheon Company patents a "high-frequency dielectric heating apparatus," otherwise known as a microwave oven.

1953: The first heart-lung machine, which takes over the functions of these vital organs, is used during an operation.

1953: The Department of Health, Education, and Welfare is created as part of the U.S. president's cabinet.

1953: IBM introduces its first computer, the 701.

1953: *Playboy* (1953–) becomes the first mass-market men's magazine and rockets to popularity when it publishes nude pictures of rising movie star Marilyn Monroe.

1953: Sara Lee Kitchens begins mass-marketing frozen cakes and pies.

1953: February 15 Tenley Albright becomes the first American to win the World Figure Skating title.

1953: April 3–9 The first national edition of *TV Guide* is published.

1953: June 11 For the first time, the Harvard University Law School awards degrees to women.

1953: **June 19** Julius and Ethel Rosenberg, convicted of passing atomic secrets to the Soviet Union, are electrocuted in Sing Sing prison in New York.

1953: **July 10** Ben Hogan takes the British Open, after already having won the Masters and the U.S. Open, making him the first golfer ever to win all three major championships in the same year.

1953: **July 27** An armistice, or peace agreement, is signed ending the Korean War.

1953: **October 5** The New York Yankees become the first team ever to win five consecutive World Series.

1954: Bell Laboratories develops the photovoltaic cell, which converts sunlight into electricity.

1954: Full-scale open-heart surgery is introduced.

1954: **March** The world's largest shopping center, featuring one hundred stores, opens in Detroit, Michigan.

1954: **April 22** Senator Joseph McCarthy conducts televised hearings on supposed communist infiltration of the U.S. Army.

1954: **May 17** The landmark *Brown* v. *Board of Education of Topeka, Kansas* Supreme Court decision overrules the "separate but equal" doctrine; segregated public schools are judged to be unconstitutional.

1954: **June 14** President Dwight Eisenhower signs a bill revising the pledge of allegiance to include the words "under God," after "one nation."

1954: **August 16** The first issue of *Sports Illustrated* magazine hits the newsstands.

1954: **September 27** *The Tonight Show* (1954–) debuts on NBC.

1955: The first successful kidney transplant is performed.

1955: **January** Contralto Marian Anderson becomes the first black singer to appear at the Metropolitan Opera.

1955: **January 19** President Eisenhower holds the first televised presidential news conference.

1955: **February 2** The American Federation of Labor (AFL) and Congress of Industrial Organizations (CIO), America's two largest labor unions, announce plans to merge.

1955: June 6–13 General Motors and Ford consent to offer laid-off workers unemployment benefits for up to twenty-six weeks.

1955: July Disneyland opens in Anaheim, California.

1955: December 1 Black American seamstress Rosa Parks is arrested for refusing to relinquish her seat on a Montgomery, Alabama, bus to a white passenger. The event sparks a bus boycott by Montgomery's black residents.

1956: The kidney dialysis machine is developed.

1956: The Mid-Oceanic Ridge, a formation of mountains and rifts that circles the world under the oceans, is discovered.

1956: June 29 Charles Dumas becomes the first person to high-jump more than seven feet.

1956: October 15 The existence of an orally administered polio vaccine, developed by Albert Sabin, is announced.

1957: Synthetic penicillin is developed.

1957: The painkilling drug Darvon is introduced.

1957: A one-minute blood test for the sexually transmitted disease syphilis is introduced.

1957: Wham-O Manufacturing introduces the hula hoop and Frisbee.

1957: May–September Evangelist Billy Graham holds a series of highly publicized revival meetings in New York's Madison Square Garden.

1957: August 29 Congress passes the Civil Rights Act of 1957, which penalizes voting rights violations.

1957: September 26 The landmark musical *West Side Story,* a modern-day adaptation of *Romeo and Juliet* by William Shakespeare, opens on Broadway at the Winter Garden Theatre.

1957: October 4 The Soviet Union launches its *Sputnik* satellite.

1958: Ultrasound examination of fetuses is introduced.

1958: The first U.S. artificial satellite orbits Earth.

1958: Bifocal contact lenses are developed.

1958: Pizza Hut opens its first restaurant in Kansas City, Missouri.

1958: October 2 Leonard Bernstein begins his first season as director of the New York Philharmonic.

1959: Sony produces the initial transistorized black-and-white television set in the United States.

1959: The pressure test for glaucoma is developed.

1959: A combined vaccine for whooping cough, diphtheria, and polio is made available.

1959: A resuscitator small enough to be used on infants is developed.

1959: **February 3** Rock and roll legends Buddy Holly, Ritchie Valens, and J. P. Richardson, known as "The Big Bopper," die in a plane crash outside Clear Lake, Iowa.

1959: **April 25** The Saint Lawrence Seaway, an engineering marvel that provides sea access from the Atlantic Ocean to the Great Lakes, opens to shipping.

1959: **August 21** Hawaii becomes America's fiftieth state.

1959: **October 21** The Solomon R. Guggenheim Museum, designed by architect Frank Lloyd Wright, opens in New York.

The 1950s: An Overview

The 1950s was a time of great prosperity and growth in the United States. During most of the decade, the economy boomed. Jobs were numerous, while unions negotiated pay raises for their employees. Blue collar workers in particular enjoyed unheard-of affluence. They purchased homes and automobiles, and entered the middle class. Veterans of World War II (1939–45) were marrying and starting families. They abandoned America's cities and sought out recently constructed and expanded suburban communities. America increasingly became a nation in motion. Cars clogged the country's newly constructed superhighways, and a modern roadside landscape of motels and fast-food restaurants emerged. When not out driving, Americans gathered around their newly purchased television sets. During the 1950s, TV became a major force in American culture as each week millions shared the experience of laughing along with Lucille Ball (1911–1989), Milton Berle (1908–2002), Sid Caesar (1922–), and other legends of early television.

Meanwhile, spectacular advances were made in the detection and cure of illness. In particular, vaccines were discovered that were antidotes to polio, a dreaded disease that had paralyzed the bodies of thousands. Scientific and technological progress made everyday life more pleasant and comfortable. Jet-propelled aircraft and transatlantic telephone cables became the facts of real life, rather than fantasies that might have been conjured up by science fiction writers. Most far-reaching of all, perhaps, was the marketing of the world's first commercial computer, the UNIVAC I.

Much to their parent's dismay, many teenagers embraced a new kind of music, called rock and roll. While adults found the music loud and abrasive, young people found it liberating. Children welcomed the era's fads. In mid-decade, they wore coonskin caps. Near the end, they played with hula hoops. Architectural design was spare and functional, while abstract expressionist paintings dominated the art world. Baseball remained America's National Pastime, and three New York-based teams—the Brooklyn Dodgers, the New York Giants, and, in particular, the New York Yankees—ruled the major leagues.

On the political front, the Republicans reigned in the White House. Dwight Eisenhower (1890–1969), a hero of World War II, was elected president in 1952 and reelected in 1956. His grandfatherly presence made him the era's ideal American political leader.

Since the abolition of slavery almost one hundred years earlier, black Americans had remained second-class citizens. The U.S. Supreme Court, in its 1954 *Brown v. Board of Education of Topeka, Kansas* decision, ruled that separate schools for black and white children did not constitute equality under the law. It was a landmark case that helped to usher in the Civil Rights movement.

On the international stage, the decade began with the United States immersed in a shooting war against the communist North Koreans and Chinese in what became known as the Korean War (1950–53). By then, the cold war—a struggle that pitted democracy against communism—was raging between the United States and Soviet Union, the world's two superpowers. While it was a bloodless war, the threat of an all-out nuclear showdown remained ever-present. The launching of the *Sputnik* satellite by the Soviet Union in 1957 further escalated the cold war, and thrust the United States into the space age. Fear of communism also translated into a "Red Scare," which enveloped the country. Joseph McCarthy (1909–1957), the junior senator from Wisconsin, grabbed power by haphazardly accusing Americans of communist affiliations. During the decade, nuclear technology was developed and tested, and a debate raged over how that technology would be employed. Would it be used for peaceful purposes, or as a weapon of war that someday might destroy civilization?

Arts and Entertainment

1950: March The Boston Institute of Contemporary Art and New York's Metropolitan Museum and Whitney Museum release a joint Statement on Modern Art opposing "any attempt to make art or opinion about art conform to a single point of view."

1950: October 2 *Peanuts,* the comic strip written and drawn by Charles Schulz, debuts in seven U.S. newspapers.

1951: *The Caine Mutiny,* the war novel by Herman Wouk, is published and soon becomes one of the longest-lasting bestsellers of all time, holding its place on the *New York Times* list for forty-eight weeks.

1951: August 5 The soap operas *Search for Tomorrow* (1951–82) and *Love of Life* (1951–80) premiere on CBS.

1951: October 15 The sitcom *I Love Lucy* (1951–57) premieres on CBS.

1951: November 18 The news program *See It Now* (1951–58), hosted by Edward R. Murrow, premieres on CBS.

1952: *Gunsmoke* debuts as a radio drama. In 1955, the Western drama moves to TV where it lasts until 1975. The show becomes the longest running prime-time TV show with continuing characters.

1952: January *American Bandstand* (1952–89), a popular teen-oriented music program, debuts as a local show in Philadelphia. Dick Clark, its most famous host, comes aboard in 1956.

1952: January 14 *The Today Show* (1952–) debuts on NBC.

1952: November *Bwana Devil,* the first 3-D movie, is released.

1953: *Playboy* (1953–) becomes the first mass-market men's magazine and rockets to popularity when it publishes nude pictures of rising movie star Marilyn Monroe.

1953: January 1 Hank Williams, the father of contemporary country music, dies at age twenty-nine from a heart disease resulting from excessive drinking.

1953: April 3–9 The first national edition of *TV Guide* is published.

1954: April 4 Walt Disney signs a contract with ABC to produce twenty-six television films each year.

1954: **July** The Newport Jazz Festival debuts in Newport, Rhode Island.

1954: **July 19** "That's All Right, Mama" and "Blue Moon of Kentucky," the first professional records made by Elvis Presley, are released on Sun Records.

1954: **September 27** *The Tonight Show* (1954–) debuts on NBC.

1955: *The $64,000 Question* (1955–58) debuts and soon becomes the most popular game show of the 1950s.

1955: **January** Contralto Marian Anderson becomes the first black singer to appear at the Metropolitan Opera.

1955: **January 19** President Dwight Eisenhower holds the first televised presidential news conference.

1955: **March** *The Blackboard Jungle,* the first feature film to include a rock and roll song on its soundtrack, "Rock Around the Clock," by Bill Haley and The Comets, opens. The song becomes the country's number-one single in July.

1955: **September 30** Actor James Dean dies after his Porsche roadster slams into another car on a California highway.

1955: **October 13** Poet Allen Ginsberg gives the first public reading of *Howl,* his controversial poem-in-progress.

1956: **November 30** Videotape is first used commercially on television, during the broadcast of CBS' *Douglas Edwards with the News* (1948–62).

1957: **September 26** The landmark musical *West Side Story,* a modern-day adaptation of *Romeo and Juliet* by William Shakespeare, opens on Broadway at the Winter Garden Theatre.

1958: **October 2** Leonard Bernstein begins his first season as director of the New York Philharmonic.

1958: **October 16** Sponsors drop the NBC quiz show *Twenty-One* (1956–58) after a grand jury investigation determines that contestants were provided with preshow answers.

1959: **February 3** Rock and roll legends Buddy Holly, Ritchie Valens, and J. P. Richardson, otherwise known as "The Big Bopper," die in a plane crash outside Clear Lake, Iowa.

1959: **October 21** The Solomon R. Guggenheim Museum, designed by architect Frank Lloyd Wright, opens in New York.

Overview

The 1950s was the decade in which television emerged as the dominating force in American entertainment—a standing that remains to this day. The veterans of World War II were marrying, starting families, and migrating from the city to the suburbs. Pulling up a chair, flicking on a TV set, and being entertained by Milton Berle, Sid Caesar, Lucille Ball, Jackie Gleason, and other first-generation TV stars was more convenient and less costly than hiring a babysitter and trekking off to the motion picture palace. A host of now-legendary television shows debuted, and many top movie personalities who initially resisted the call of television eventually began appearing on the small screen.

As Americans purchased TV sets by the millions, movie ticket sales plummeted. In order to lure back customers, the motion picture industry employed a range of gimmicks, including 3-D and wide-screen processes. While character- and plot-driven stories still made their way to the big screen, historical epics featuring state-of-the-art special effects and enormous casts of actors and extras became the decade's most prominent films.

A new generation of actors also emerged, with many—Marlon Brando (1924–) is perhaps the most famous—embracing "method" acting, an approach that emphasized inner motivation, feeling, and emotion over dramatic performance. Meanwhile, scores of names familiar to moviegoers no longer could be found in big-screen credits. These individuals had been blacklisted for refusing to cooperate with the House Un-American Activities Committee (HUAC), a congressional committee investigating alleged communist influence in the entertainment industry.

In the art world, paintings generally were composed of fewer recognizable objects. Realist artworks were out of favor, and the most notable artworks were abstract. The decade's major art-world names were such innovative abstract expressionists/action painters as Jackson Pollock and Willem de Kooning. Art critics were divided over the merits of this trend, while museum-goers often were perplexed by paintings that bore no relation to the world most people experienced.

With regard to literature, such veteran writers as William Faulkner and Ernest Hemingway published new works, while a host of younger literary voices emerged. None were more controversial than such nonconformist, Beat Generation writers as Jack Kerouac and Allen Ginsberg, whose creations were sexually charged and decidedly antiestablishment. One of the decade's major trends was an increase of interest in science fiction literature, which, not surprisingly, was linked to the advent of the Atomic Age in science and technology.

On the popular music front, adults in the mainstream generally favored sounds that were sedate and refined, upbeat and dreamily romantic: songs that originated on Broadway, for example, or the stylings of Frank Sinatra, Perry Como, Dinah Shore, Dean Martin, and Nat King Cole. Yet their adolescent sons and daughters took to the strong beat and rebellious attitude of rock and roll. The adult establishment criticized rock and roll music because it was loud, unsophisticated, and rooted in African American country blues and urban rhythm and blues. Despite their disdain, rock and roll was here to stay. Its popularity revolutionized the music industry.

Milton Berle (1908–2002) In the summer of 1948, Milton Berle was a veteran vaudeville, radio, nightclub, and film performer who had never quite attained major stardom. He was signed by NBC to make several appearances on *The Texaco Star Theater* (1948–53), a new variety show. Berle was an immediate hit and, in September, became the program's permanent host. He was beloved for his noisy comedy routines, his contagious laughter during these skits, and his outrageous costumes. He was America's first great television star. He is fondly remembered as "Uncle Miltie" and "Mr. Television." **Photo reproduced by permission of Archive Photos, Inc.**

Leonard Bernstein (1918–1990) Leonard Bernstein was a man of many talents: a symphony composer and conductor, concert pianist, impresario (a director of a concert company), teacher, and composer of music for stage and screen. During the 1950s, he scored the music for the classic film *On the Waterfront* (1954) and collaborated on two celebrated Broadway stage productions, *Candide* (1956) and *West Side Story* (1957). In 1958 Bernstein became music director of the New York Philharmonic, as well as the orchestra's resident conductor. Most prominent of all, perhaps, was his knack for making classical music appealing to audiences of all ages. **Photo reproduced by permission of the Estate of Carl Van Vechten.**

Marlon Brando (1924–) Marlon Brando was the foremost practitioner of "method acting" during the 1950s. He started out on the stage, winning instant fame in 1947 with his legendary performance as the brutish Stanley Kowalski in *A Streetcar Named Desire*. He recreated the role in the 1951 screen version, and earned an Academy Award playing an angst-ridden longshoreman in *On the Waterfront* (1954). Other celebrated Brando roles include a rebellious, leather jacket-clad motorcycle gang leader in *The Wild One* (1954) and Mafia boss Don Corleone in *The Godfather* (1972). **Photo reproduced courtesy of the Library of Congress.**

Jack Kerouac (1922–1969) Of all the novelists who earned fame during the 1950s, Jack Kerouac stands out because of the type of books he wrote, as well as his writing style. Both may be best described as spontaneous and free-spirited. In *On the Road* (1957), his landmark novel that became the Beat Generation bible, Kerouac's words flow in a stream-of-consciousness manner. His nonconformist characters, based on the lives of the author and his peers, strike out on their own and trek across America on odysseys of self-discovery. **Photo reproduced by permission of Mr. Jerry Bauer.**

Marilyn Monroe (1926–1962) Marilyn Monroe was the premier Hollywood movie star and sex symbol of the 1950s. However, she was no mere beauty who maintained her stardom simply by posing. She was a serious actress and superb comedienne, whose talents, sadly, were overlooked during her lifetime. Her acting skill was recognized only after her tragic death at age thirty-seven from an overdose of barbiturates. The vision of Monroe standing over a New York City subway grate in *The Seven-Year Itch* (1955), with a gust of wind causing her dress to billow above her waist, remains one of the decade's enduring pop-culture images.

Photo reproduced by permission of Archive Photos, Inc.

Edward R. Murrow (1908–1965) Edward R. Murrow was a respected journalist who practically invented radio and television news reporting. He first earned fame during World War II (1939–45) with his radio broadcasts from London during the Battle of Britain. Murrow's two important 1950s television shows were *Person to Person* (1953–61), on which he visited the homes of public figures, and *See It Now* (1952–55), on which he reported on public issues. His news reports, from his sobering coverage of the Korean War to his defiant exposé of the trickery of Senator Joseph McCarthy (1908–1957), made him a television legend. *Photo reproduced by permission of the Corbis Corporation.*

Jackson Pollock (1912–1956) Although he died halfway through the decade, Jackson Pollock was the 1950s' most successful and notorious abstract expressionist painter. His most famous works are enormous drip paintings consisting of layers of multicolored splashes. During the last half-decade of his life, no American artist won as much popular attention as Pollock. However, he was just as legendary for his boorish and abusive behavior and his fondness for alcohol. He died at age forty-four while on a drinking binge when the car he was driving veered off a winding road near his studio in East Hampton, Long Island. *Photo reproduced by permission of Artists Rights Society, Inc.*

Elvis Presley (1935–1977) Elvis Presley was the first great 1950s rock and roll star. Countless teenage girls panted when Presley shook his hips, snarled, and belted out "Hound Dog" and "Jailhouse Rock" or crooned "Love Me Tender," three of his early hits. In 1956, RCA-Victor sold ten million Presley "singles" (also known as 45s or 45-rpm records; these were small vinyl records with one song recorded on each side). However, two years later, Elvis was drafted into the U.S. Army. While he remained a star for the rest of his life, he no longer was the unbridled, premilitary "Elvis the Pelvis." *Photo reproduced by permission of Archive Photos, Inc.*

Topics in the News

❖ ABSTRACT EXPRESSIONISM CONFUSES ART PATRONS

During the 1950s, a new kind of art, known as "abstract expressionism" and "action painting," revolutionized the art world. Since the heyday of the late nineteenth-century French impressionists—artists like Edgar Degas (1834–1917), Edouard Manet (1833–1883), Claude Monet (1840–1926), Camille Pissarro (1830–1903), and Pierre-Auguste Renoir (1841–1919), who reproduced impressions of subjects without much focus on detail— paintings in general had included fewer recognizable objects. Line, color, and composition were being used to express mood; some paintings were solely comprised of color schemes, geometric shapes, or drips and blobs of paint. Occasionally, recognizable forms might be contained within the painting, but the image on the canvas often was completely abstract.

The art that qualifies as "action painting" expressed the feeling and power of abstract painting. Jackson Pollock (1912–1956), who today is arguably the most celebrated of all action painters, emphasized the spontaneity and physical act of creating art by splashing and dripping paint onto his canvasses. Willem de Kooning (1904–1997) used thick globs of paint to create both semifigurative and abstract works. Franz Kline (1910–1962) produced large black-and-white canvases. The paintings of Hans Hofmann (1880–1966) were dynamic and colorful. The works of Robert Motherwell (1915–) were characterized by large indistinct shapes, some of which resembled inkblots. Mark Rothko (1903–1970) used a range of colors to create simple designs, often emphasizing large, rectangular shapes.

To the casual museum-goer who preferred representational paintings, or at least impressionistic images of recognizable objects, abstract expressionism was confusing and annoying. To them, action paintings were nonpaintings, and their creators were nonartists. However, those who objected to abstract art generally did not consider the artists' individual objectives and the intellectual and physical effort that went into creating the art.

❖ IN LITERATURE, THE OLD MEETS THE NEW

The 1950s not only saw a number of established American writers publishing major works, but also gave rise to a new generation of writers who challenged Americans to develop new literary tastes. A number of novels published during the decade have become American fiction classics, including *The Martian Chronicles* (1950), by Ray Bradbury (1920–); *From Here to Eternity* (1951), by James Jones (1921–1977); *The Old Man*

During the 1950s, no living artist won more critical attention than Willem de Kooning (1904–1997) — not even his friend and rival, Jackson Pollock (1912–1956). On three occasions, de Kooning's works were included in Italy's Venice Biennale, the most prestigious international contemporary art exhibition. Seven times, they were displayed in the Whitney Museum's Annual Exhibition of Contemporary American Painting. De Kooning's works were the centerpiece of the Guggenheim Museum's influential Young American Painters exhibit. His three one-man shows at Manhattan's Sidney Janis Gallery were among the most prominent of the decade.

and the Sea (1952), by Ernest Hemingway (1899–1961); *Breakfast at Tiffany's* (1958), by Truman Capote (1924–1984); and *Goodbye, Columbus* (1959), by Philip Roth (1933–). However, if one had to cite the decade's most celebrated novel, a worthy choice would be *The Catcher in the Rye* (1951), by J. D. Salinger (1919–), a first-person narrative about Holden Caulfield, a disillusioned adolescent. The book was controversial for its cynicism, raw language, and preoccupation with sex. Yet Caulfield became an instant spokesperson for his generation. For decades, his story has remained a favorite among young people.

William Faulkner (1897–1962), regarded today as one of the twentieth-century's great American writers, produced two hotly debated works in the 1950s. *A Requiem for a Nun* (1951), a sequel to his 1931 novel *Sanctuary*, featured an experimental dramatic structure that confused readers, unsure if it was a play or a novel. *A Fable* (1954), his story of a French army officer who reenacts the Passion of Christ, was labeled by some reviewers as "remarkable" and "extraordinary," while others called it "spurious and unreal," "a heroically ambitious failure," and a "bad small novel."

The decade also saw the rise of a new generation of nonconformist Beat Generation writers, including novelist Jack Kerouac (1922–1969) and poet Allen Ginsberg (1926–1997), who aroused controversy for their emphasis on spiritual values over physical comfort and the pursuit of wealth, the sexual nature of their work, and their experimental writing styles. Because of its sexual content, *Howl and Other Poems* (1956), Ginsberg's lone work published during the decade, was seized by officials and

Pulitzer Prize Winners in Fiction in the 1950s

Year	Title	Author
1950	*The Way West*	A. B. Guthrie
1951	*The Town*	Conrad Richter
1952	*The Caine Mutiny*	Herman Wouk
1953	*The Old Man and the Sea*	Ernest Hemingway
1954	no award	
1955	*A Fable*	William Faulkner
1956	*Andersonville*	MacKinlay Kantor
1957	no award	
1958	*A Death in the Family*	James Agee
1959	*The Travels of Jaimie McPheeters*	Robert Lewis Taylor

dubbed obscene. A highly publicized trial followed, ending in a victory for free speech with the acquittal of its publisher, poet Lawrence Ferlinghetti (1920–). During this decade, William S. Burroughs (1914–1997) also published his controversial novel *Naked Lunch* (1959).

The sales of paperback books, small-size, low-cost alternatives to hardcover editions, increased during the 1950s. Some books came out first in hardcover and then were published in paperback, while others went directly to paperback. Unlike hardcover books, which were sold only in bookstores, the smaller, inexpensive paperback could be sold in a range of venues, from newsstands to low-priced "five-and-dime" stores.

❖ MOVIES REACT TO THE RISE OF TV

The motion picture industry underwent a major overhaul during the 1950s. As television set sales steadily increased, more Americans chose to stay home and watch free television rather than go out to the movies. As a result, box-office receipts plummeted. In order to lure audiences back into theaters, the motion picture industry employed a range of gimmicks. One of the most famous was the short-lived 3-D process, used in such films as *Bwana Devil* (1952), *House of Wax* (1953), and *Kiss Me Kate* (1953). Films shot in 3-D were viewed with special glasses, creating the illusion of three-dimensional photography.

Movie producers decided that another way to challenge television would be to create lavish productions that were too expensive for TV programmers to copy. The studios began offering more and more spectacles: big-budget, special effects-laden swashbucklers, biblical epics, and costume dramas featuring "casts of thousands." Among these movies were *Quo Vadis?* (1951), *The Robe* (1953), *The Ten Commandments* (1956), and *The Buccaneer* (1958). A range of films were shot using such wide-screen processes as CinemaScope, Cinerama, and VistaVision.

The popularity of television during the decade also resulted in the demise of the Hollywood studio system. Previously, the major studios and their top executives ruled the industry. Actors, directors, producers, and writers signed standard, seven-year contracts, and they had no choice but to comply with the wishes of their bosses. Now, with the decline in power of the studio, actors began forming their own production companies, selecting their own projects, and bargaining for their films' financing and distribution rights.

Previously, most Hollywood films were shot on the soundstages of M-G-M, Warner Bros., or Columbia Pictures. Locations from a New York street to a Paris nightclub to an African village were recreated on studio lots. Now, however, films were increasingly being shot on location, with filmmakers adding authenticity to their work by bringing their actors and cameras directly to avenues, cafés, and villages across the globe.

During the decade, more Americans were driving cars. This increased mobility also impacted the motion picture industry by boosting the popularity of the drive-in theater. There, audiences could remain in their cars as they watched movies on a wide screen.

An audience watching a 3-D (three-dimensional) movie. The motion picture industry employed such gimmicks to lure customers away from television. **Courtesy of the Library of Congress.**

Marilyn Monroe, Tony Curtis, and Jack Lemmon on the set of the popular film comedy Some Like It Hot. ***Reproduced by permission of the Kobal Collection.***

"Method" acting also came to the forefront during the 1950s. The Method, emphasized inner motivation and anguish over dramatic performance. Marlon Brando (1924–), James Dean (1931–1955), and Montgomery Clift (1920–1966) were three of the decade's top movie stars who espoused The Method.

Best Picture Academy Award Winners

Year	Film
1950	*All About Eve*
1951	*An American in Paris*
1952	*The Greatest Show on Earth*
1953	*From Here to Eternity*
1954	*On the Waterfront*
1955	*Marty*
1956	*Around the World in 80 Days*
1957	*The Bridge on the River Kwai*
1958	*Gigi*
1959	*Ben-Hur*

Among the decade's other major stars were Elizabeth Taylor, Rock Hudson, Debbie Reynolds, Audrey Hepburn, Marilyn Monroe, Doris Day, Grace Kelly, Gary Cooper, John Wayne, James Stewart, William Holden, and the comedy team of Dean Martin and Jerry Lewis.

❖ THE HOLLYWOOD BLACKLIST

During the 1930s, Americans were suffering through the Great Depression. Many individuals who cared about others and felt disheartened by the suffering around them felt that the American economic system had failed. Some joined the Communist Party. Others simply were concerned about their country's future.

After World War II (1939–45) came the advent of the cold war. The Union of Soviet Socialist Republics—U.S.S.R., or Soviet Union—a communist bloc of nations best known by the name of its dominant country, Russia, had been one of America's allies during World War II. Now it was an enemy of the United States, and many Americans feared the influence of communists. A congressional committee, known as the House Un-American Activities Committee (HUAC), began investigating alleged communist influence in the motion picture industry.

When they were called before the committee, witnesses were asked, "Are you now, or have you ever been, a member of the Communist Party?"

Elia Kazan and Lillian Hellman

In 1954, *On the Waterfront* earned an Academy Award as the year's best picture. It is the story of Terry Malloy (played by Marlon Brando [1924–]), a young dockworker who struggles with his conscience when he is subpoenaed to testify before a crime commission investigating waterfront gangsters.

The film's director, Elia Kazan (1909–), and its screenwriter, Budd Schulberg (1914–), previously had testified before HUAC, and both had chosen to "name names." Kazan claimed he cooperated because he felt that communism was an evil which needed to be exposed and destroyed. Others believed that he and Schulberg complied solely to avoid blacklisting and save their careers.

The story told in *One the Waterfront* serves as a rebuttal to Kazan's and Schulberg's critics. In their film, Terry testifies against thugs who are clearly defined villains. He is doing the right thing, just as Kazan and Schulberg claimed they had done by cooperating with HUAC.

Kazan's and Schulberg's actions may be contrasted to the decision made by playwright Lillian Hellman (1905–1984) not to "name names." In a letter she sent to HUAC before her testimony, she declared that, "...to hurt innocent people whom I knew many years ago in order to save myself is, to me, inhuman and indecent and dishonorable. I cannot and will not cut my conscience to fit this year's fashions...."

Answering "yes" was not enough to satisfy the HUAC questioners, however. Witnesses were expected to further cleanse themselves by "naming names" of other so-called "guilty parties." It did not matter that the committee might already be in possession of these names. The purpose was to embarrass witnesses by compelling them to snitch publicly on their colleagues and friends.

Many refused to comply with HUAC because of their belief that, in America, one's political affiliation is a private affair. Yet given the mood of the era, anyone who refused to testify could be held in contempt of Congress. Furthermore, they almost certainly would be blacklisted, which meant that they could no longer find employment in the movie industry. During the 1950s, scores of Hollywood directors, producers, actors, and writers were blacklisted. Careers were ruined and friendships were destroyed.

Many screenwriters managed to keep working, but did not earn on-screen acknowledgment for their scripts. Instead, they were given fictitious names, or nonblacklisted writers were credited. The beginning of the end of the blacklist came at the decade's close, when actor and producer Kirk Douglas (1916–) and director Otto Preminger (1905–1986) insisted that the blacklisted writer Dalton Trumbo (1905–1976) receive full credit for the screenplays that he had written for their respective films, *Spartacus* (1960) and *Exodus* (1960).

❖ THE BIRTH OF ROCK AND ROLL

The 1950s saw the evolution of two styles of music that were distinctly American: modern jazz and rock and roll. The experimental, free-form stylings of such jazz legends as Charlie Parker, Dizzy Gillespie, Thelonious Monk, Dave Brubeck, Oscar Peterson, Gerry Mulligan, and Miles Davis almost exclusively appealed to a small but fervent audience of intellectual hipsters. However, rock and roll was a different story altogether, with its mass popularity revolutionizing the recording industry.

Before such rock performers as Chuck Berry, Little Richard, Elvis Presley, Jerry Lee Lewis, and Fats Domino invaded the radio airwaves, popular music was more sedate. The era's singing stars—including Frank Sinatra, Perry Como, Dinah Shore, Dean Martin, and Nat King Cole—were older, more traditional performers whose brand of sophisticated, romantic music appealed to adults. Adolescents viewed these artists as too slow and inhibited. Rock music, on the other hand, required neither complex instrumentation nor refined lyrics, and was ruled by basic chords and simple melodies and arrangements. In order to rock, all a band required was a singer, rhythm guitarist, bass guitarist, and drummer. The sound of the music, its beat and sheer loudness, was what made it so appealing. Lyrics and voice quality were secondary to emotion and feeling.

When kids listened to rock and roll, they felt free to express themselves on the dance floor—enthusiastically. This freedom, combined with the fact that much of rock and roll was rooted in African American rural blues and urban rhythm and blues, made it controversial in white, middle-class circles. Some parents, politicians, and educators viewed rock and roll as downright sinful. Back in 1956, the image of a white fifteen-year-old girl gyrating to the sounds of black soloists and singing groups was scandalous. Rock and roll's most vocal critics called it a communist plot, and certainly a sign of the downfall of civilization.

The popularity of rock and roll was viewed by many as a fad. Antirock and roll forces hoped that Elvis Presley's 1958 entry into the U.S. Army would signal the beginning of the end for the music. By then, however, rock and roll had irreversibly entered the mainstream of American culture.

❖ THE RISE OF SCIENCE FICTION

Paralleling the birth of the Atomic Age, with its jet engines and atom bombs, came an avid interest in science fiction (sci-fi). Increasingly, writers concocted stories about rocket ships flying to the moon, aliens living on faraway planets, aliens coming to Earth, or nuclear experiments gone awry. These writers found a ready audience for their fantastic speculations.

Previously, science fiction literature had been highly structured, with storylines following standard formulas. Most sci-fi stories were short and were published in magazines. In 1945, nine science-fiction magazines were published in the United States. By 1953, the number had increased to fifty-three, and sci-fi comic books were flooding the marketplace. This exposure led several paperback publishing houses, including Ace and Ballantine, to publish short story anthologies and single-author novels. A generation of sci-fi writers began earning accolades during the 1950s, including Isaac Asimov, Ray Bradbury, Robert A. Heinlein, Theodore Sturgeon, and A. E. Van Vogt.

The movie industry also joined the sci-fi bandwagon. A few films, such as *The Thing* (1951), *The Day the Earth Stood Still* (1951), *When Worlds Collide* (1951), and *The War of the Worlds* (1953), were ambitious, high-prestige productions. Most, though, were made on small budgets and emphasized melodrama over plot.

During the early 1950s, as television sets began selling as quickly as hot dogs at a baseball park, a market emerged for a weekly publication that offered viewers an easily accessible program schedule. That publication became *TV Guide,* first issued nationally in 1953.

Over the decades, *TV Guide* has printed feature articles on TV shows and stars, series reviews, and TV-oriented gossip. However, its primary appeal is still its television schedule, which makes it an essential weekly purchase for millions of viewers and a fixture alongside the family TV set.

Television united with science fiction in the series *Tales of Tomorrow* (1951– 1953), which featured adult-oriented stories of the supernatural. Then in 1959 came the debut of *The Twilight Zone* (1959–1965), a fantasy-oriented dramatic anthology that won a large, loyal audience.

❖ THE TELEVISION DECADE

The 1950s was the decade of television, with TV-watching replacing radio listening and movie-going as America's favorite entertainment activity. In 1946, approximately 7,000 television sets had been purchased in the United States. Two years later, the number had increased to 172,000. By 1950, it had risen to 5,000,000. By the end of the decade, 90 percent of all American homes were equipped with at least one TV set.

The motion picture industry initially looked down on television, viewing it as an inferior form of entertainment. However, as more Americans purchased sets and programming expanded, movie stars reluctantly began appearing on television. A new generation of stars also emerged on this new medium, ranging from comic actors (Milton Berle, Jackie Gleason, Danny Thomas, Sid Caesar, Lucille Ball, Desi Arnaz) to talk-and variety-show hosts (Ed Sullivan, Steve Allen, Jack Paar, Art Linkletter) and unconventional innovators (Ernie Kovacs). Occasionally, actors who first had won fame on television series—including Steve McQueen (1930–1980), the star of *Wanted: Dead or Alive* (1958–61), and Clint Eastwood (1930–), featured on *Rawhide* (1959–66)—later graduated to big-screen stardom. Meanwhile, more Americans began to depend on television for news. Such TV journalists and news anchors as Edward R. Murrow, Chet Huntley, David Brinkley, Walter Cronkite, Charles Collingwood, and Eric Sevareid became famous faces as well as household names.

Today, all network TV series are filmed or taped, as were many of the 1950s programs. However, back then, a number of shows, including *The Colgate Comedy Hour* (1950–55), *Studio One* (1948–58), and *The Alcoa Hour* (1955–57), were broadcast live. Performers pranced about in comedy skits or acted out a range of emotions, with their performances broadcast into millions of homes as they occurred.

A range of 1950s television programs are fondly recalled today. During the decade, such classic situation comedies as *The Adventures of Ozzie & Harriet* (1952–66), *Leave It to Beaver* (1957–63), and *Father Knows Best* (1954–63) featured comfortable middle-class characters. *The Honeymooners* (1955–56) was a happy exception. Its characters were strictly blue collar: big-mouthed bus driver Ralph Kramden (Jackie Gleason [1916–1987]); dumb but lovable sewer worker Ed Norton (Art Carney [1918–]), and wives Alice Kramden (Audrey Meadows [1922–1996]) and Trixie Norton (Joyce Randolph [1925–]). All were recognizable to viewers who regularly struggled to pay their bills and realize their modest American dreams.

Variety shows were also popular during the 1950s. Singers Perry Como (1912–2001) and Dinah Shore (1916–1994) hosted their own programs, on

Cast members from The Honeymooners, *one of the most popular television shows of the 1950s. From left to right: Jackie Gleason, Art Carney, Audrey Meadows, and Joyce Randolph.*
Reproduced by permission of Archive Photos, Inc.

which they sang, joked, and introduced guest performers. *The Ed Sullivan Show* (1948–71), originally known as *Toast of the Town*, became a Sunday night staple. Its host, Ed Sullivan, was a former newspaper columnist whose legendary stiffness won him the nickname "The Great Stone Face." Nonetheless, Sullivan (1901–1974) was a master showman who welcomed a breathtaking range of performers, including show business legends, classical musicians, rock and roll acts, magicians, tightrope artists, and dancing bears.

Quiz shows also captivated audiences in the 1950s. Among the primetime hits were *The $64,000 Question* (1955–58) and *Twenty-One* (1956–58), on which contestants won money by displaying their knowledge. However, at the end of the decade, a quiz show scandal erupted, with show producers accused of providing contestants with answers beforehand.

Not all classic TV shows aired during prime time. Two of the most celebrated programs of the 1950s, in fact, continued to be broadcast into the twenty-first century. *The Today Show* (1952–) was America's first national early morning program. It featured news summaries, sports and weather reports, and interviews. To date, *Today* has logged more on-air hours than any show in television history. *The Tonight Show* (1954–) aired in the late evening, after the local news. Its first host was Steve Allen (1921–2000). From the beginning, *The Tonight Show* featured celebrity chatter, music, jokes, comedy sketches, and guest stars.

Of all the vintage 1950s television shows, perhaps the most beloved is *I Love Lucy* (1951–1957). This laugh-out-loud situation comedy spotlighted four characters: zany Lucy Ricardo (Lucille Ball [1911–1989]), who yearns for a show business career; her Cuban-born bandleader husband Ricky (Desi Arnaz [1917–1986]); and their neighbors, landlords, and partners in comedy, Fred and Ethel Mertz (William Frawley [1887–1966] and Vivian Vance [1909–1979]). *I Love Lucy* is notable for more than its timeless humor. The show was groundbreaking in that it was filmed, rather than broadcast live, resulting in top-quality archive film reels that have been rebroadcast for decades around the world.

For More Information

BOOKS

Andrews, Bart. *The "I Love Lucy" Book*. Garden City, NY: Doubleday, 1985.

Aronson, Marc. *Art Attack: A Short Cultural History of the Avant-Garde*. New York: Clarion Books, 1998.

Bergamini, Andrea. *The History of Rock Music*. Hauppauge, NY: Barron's, 2000.

Arts and Entertainment

FOR MORE INFORMATION

Berke, Sally. *When TV Began: The First TV Shows.* New York: CPI, 1978.

Brooks, Tim. *The Complete Dictionary of Prime Time TV Stars.* New York: Ballantine Books, 1987.

Brooks, Tim, and Earle Marsh. *The Complete Directory to Prime Time Network and Cable TV Shows.* 4th ed. New York: Ballantine Books, 1999.

Calabro, Marian. *Zap!: A Brief History of Television.* New York: Maxwell Macmillan International, 1992.

Clifford, Mike. *The Illustrated History of Black Music.* New York: Harmony Books, 1982.

Daily, Robert. *Elvis Presley: The King of Rock 'n' Roll.* New York: Franklin Watts, 1996.

Denenberg, Barry. *All Shook Up! The Life and Death of Elvis Presley.* New York: Scholastic Press, 2001.

Epstein, Dan. *The 50s (20th Century Pop Culture).* Broomall, PA: Chelsea House, 2000.

Falkenburg, Claudia, and Andrew Solt. *A Really Big Show: A Visual History of the Ed Sullivan Show.* New York: Viking Studio Books, 1992.

Fidelman, Geoffrey Mark. *The Lucy Book.* Los Angeles: Renaissance Books, 1999.

Finkelstein, Norman H. *With Heroic Truth: The Life of Edward R. Murrow.* New York: Clarion Books, 1997.

Gourley, Catherine. *Media Wizards: A Behind-the-Scenes Look at Media Manipulations.* Brookfield, CT: Twenty-First Century Books, 1999.

Gourse, Leslie. *Blowing on the Changes: The Art of the Jazz Horn Players.* New York: Franklin Watts, 1997.

Halliwell, Sarah, ed. *The 20th Century: Post-1945 Artists, Writers, and Composers.* Austin, TX: Raintree Steck-Vaughn, 1998.

Katz, Ephraim. *The Film Encyclopedia.* 4th ed. New York: HarperResource, 2001.

Knapp, Ron. *American Legends of Rock.* Springfield, NJ: Enslow Publishers, 1996.

Krohn, Katherine E. *Marilyn Monroe: Norma Jean's Dream.* Minneapolis, MN: Lerner Publications, 1997.

Maltin, Leonard, ed. *Leonard Maltin's Movie Encyclopedia.* New York: Dutton, 1994.

Maltin, Leonard, ed. *Movie & Video Guide,* 22nd ed. New York: Signet, 2001.

McCrohan, Donna. *The Honeymooners' Companion: The Kramdens and the Nortons Revisited.* New York: Workman Publishing Company, 1978.

McNeil, Alex. *Total Television.* 4th ed. New York: Penguin Books, 1996.

Oleksy, Walter. *The Importance of James Dean.* San Diego: Lucent Books, 2001.

Schultz, Charles M. *Peanuts: A Golden Celebration.* New York: Harper Resource, 1999.

Shirley, David. *The History of Rock & Roll.* New York: Franklin Watts, 1987.

Vaughan, William H. T. *Encyclopedia of Artists.* New York: Oxford University Press, 2000.

WEB SITES

Cinema History: The 1950s—Focus on American Films. (accessed on August 9, 2002).

Pop Art. http://www.artchive.com/artchive/pop_art.html (accessed on August 9, 2002).

Rebels: Painters and Poets of the 1950s. http://www.npg.si.edu/exh/rebels/poets.htm (accessed on August 9, 2002).

chapter two **Business and the Economy**

1950: **January 11–March 5** Massive strikes rock the American coal industry.

1950: **February 8–9** The federal government orders motion picture companies to separate the production and distribution aspects of their business.

1950: **June 20** The housing industry reports that housing construction rose 52 percent over the same period in 1949.

1950: **August 25** President Harry S Truman directs the U.S. Army to run the nation's railroads to prevent a threatened strike by railroad unions.

1951: **April 9** The Federal Communications Commission (FCC) sanctions an agreement between American Telephone & Telegraph (AT&T) and Western Union to stay out of each other's business domain.

1951: **May 15** AT&T becomes the first American corporation with one million stockholders.

1952: **April 8** President Truman authorizes the takeover of the nation's $7 billion steel industry, to thwart a walkout by 650,000 steelworkers.

1952: **May–July 25** The steel strike ends, but workers walk out again when the U.S. Supreme Court rules that Truman's takeover was unconstitutional.

1953: **IBM introduces** its first computer the 701.

1953: **November 26** Economic growth in the United States continues to rise, increasing by 5 percent ($368 billion) over 1952.

1954: **March 9** General Motors reports $10.2 billion in sales, topping all U.S. companies.

1954: **September–October** Consumer credit increases for the sixth straight month, officially ending the recession.

1955: **February 2** The American Federation of Labor (AFL) and Congress of Industrial Organizations (CIO), America's two largest labor unions, announce plans to merge.

1955: **May 2–6** American steel companies establish a one-week record for steel production by producing 2.32 million net tons of ingots and casting.

1955: **June 6–13** General Motors and Ford both consent to offer laid-off workers unemployment benefits for up to twenty-six weeks.

1955: **July 30** Congress increases the minimum wage to $1 per hour.

1955: **October 14** The Commerce Department announces that the U.S. annual national income has risen to record levels; the Securities and Exchange

Commission reports that U.S. corporate working assets also have risen, to $100.6 billion as of June 30.

1956: March 20 The AFL-CIO and Westinghouse settle their labor controversy, ending a 156-day-long strike.

1956: June 30 The 650,000 members of the United Steelworkers of America union walk off their jobs. The strike is settled on July 27.

1956: November 4 Personal income of Americans rises to a record annual rate of $330.5 billion.

1957: May 20 The AFL-CIO ousts Teamsters Union president Dave Beck for mishandling union funds.

1957: October 7 The value of farmland rises 8 percent over the previous year, to a record $112 million.

1957: October 20 Dallas oilman H. L. Hunt is cited by the *New York Times Magazine* as the wealthiest American, with a fortune estimated at between $400 million and $700 million.

1957: December 2 The initial Westinghouse-built atomic power plant opens for business in Shippingport, Pennsylvania.

1958: March 16 The number of cars produced by the Ford Motor Company reaches the fifty-million mark.

1958: April 16 The National Highway Act is signed into law, furnishing $1.8 billion in federal spending for superhighway construction.

1958: July 16 Congress establishes the National Aeronautics and Space Administration (NASA), guaranteeing job opportunities for civilians in the burgeoning aerospace industry.

1958: December 27 Department stores report a $10 million increase in sales over 1957.

1959: January 19 President Eisenhower endorses the continuation of a 52 percent tax rate on corporate profits.

1959: May The monthly production output of steel increases to a record 11.6 million tons.

1959: July 15–December 31 The United Steelworkers of America strike at twenty-eight companies; despite intervention from President Eisenhower, the year ends without a resolution.

1959: September 29 Forty-seven percent of all Americans over the age of fourteen smoke, much to the delight of a thriving tobacco industry.

1959: October 1 Consumer credit rises to a record $47.2 billion.

✳ Overview

The American economy experienced a shift during the 1950s that created more income for more Americans than ever before. Though during the early 1950s the American economy was negatively affected by inflation—prices were rising, currency was losing its value, and a recession was at hand—these problems were relatively short-lived. By the mid-1950s, the nation began to enjoy the fruits of economic boom and prosperity. The robust economy gave rise to the American middle class.

The masses of Americans who grown up during Depression-era poverty and sacrificed for their country during World War II were now marrying, starting families, and entering the workforce. Furthermore, the GI Bill, which offered government funding for veterans attending college, allowed those who otherwise could not afford to continue their education to earn college degrees and win better-paying jobs.

During the decade, small businesses started and grew, while major corporations were merging, thus becoming larger, more profitable, and more powerful. Companies big and small needed workers, both skilled and unskilled, to manage their assets, work their assembly lines, or sell their products to the public. Jobs were readily available, and they were filled by a generation of eager-to-work veterans.

Additionally, more and more workers joined labor unions. These unions negotiated with management for pay raises, better working conditions, and health and retirement benefits. The presence and influence of unions was a key factor in allowing America's blue-collar workers to enter the middle class. A man who toiled on a factory assembly line or drove a bus or a truck for a living now had sufficient income to purchase his own home and car, not to mention the latest household appliances for his wife (who, during this prefeminist era, usually remained home and raised the children). He could take his family on vacations and save some of his weekly paychecks. However, some of the unions that represented the working man—most notoriously the International Brotherhood of Teamsters—were corrupt.

Travel became an increasingly popular pastime for many. More and more Americans drove by car long distances or boarded airplanes to fly cross-country or across the ocean. The United States was becoming a nation on wheels with a new roadside culture, and federal funds were allocated to improve the then-inadequate national highway system.

Television sets were fast becoming the centerpieces of American living rooms. With a nudge from TV advertising and its ceaseless pitches to purchase everything from beer to bathroom tissue, Americans increasingly became consumers. Of course, Americans also had purchased things in previous decades. But during the 1950s, more people had enough money to buy nonessential items, and those who didn't were making their major purchases on credit. At the same time, the commercial banking industry expanded, with insurance, trust, and holding companies also entering the money business. With the ready availability of jobs and credit, the 1950s offered most people the ability to purchase all sorts of goods and services for their material comfort.

James R. Hoffa (1913–c. 1975) James R. Hoffa is a key figure in the history of the International Brotherhood of Teamsters, the largest union in the United States. In 1957, Hoffa won the union presidency in a disputed election. However, Hoffa and his union leadership were alleged to have been linked to organized crime. In 1964, he was convicted of jury tampering, fraud, and conspiracy. Although Hoffa was jailed, he remained the union's president. In July 1975, after dining with two reputed Mafia figures, he mysteriously disappeared and eventually was declared "presumed dead." **Photo reproduced by permission of Archive Photos, Inc.**

Raymond A. Kroc (1902–1984) In 1954, Raymond A. Kroc, then the lone distributor of a multiple-milkshake-mixing machine used in restaurants, observed the operation of McDonald's, then a small-time restaurant franchise. "Visions of McDonald's restaurants dotting crossroads all over the country paraded through my brain," Kroc recalled. First he became the fast-food chain's exclusive franchising agent. Then in 1961, he purchased McDonald's for $2.7 million, and developed it into a global empire that forever altered the restaurant industry and the eating habits of millions. **Photo reproduced courtesy of the Library of Congress.**

George Meany (1894–1980) In the 1950s, the term "organized labor" was synonymous with one man: George Meany. In 1934, he became president of the New York State Federation of Labor. Five years later, he became secretary-treasurer of the American Federation of Labor (AFL). Meany was elected AFL president in 1952; three years later, he spearheaded its unification with the Congress of Industrial Organizations (CIO). He became the AFL-CIO's first president, a post he held for the next twenty-four years, during which time he engineered a campaign to rid the organization of its ties to organized crime. **Photo reproduced courtesy of the Library of Congress.**

Walter P. Reuther (1907–1970) Walter P. Reuther's organizing skills and deep commitment to the American worker made him one of the era's top labor leaders. Beginning in 1946 and ending with his death in a plane crash in 1970, Reuther was president of the United Automobile Workers (UAW). Meanwhile, in 1952, he took over leadership of the CIO. Understanding the economic, social, and political advantages of linking with the AFL, Reuther became one of the merger's most prominent supporters and planners. When the AFL and CIO emerged in 1955 as the AFL-CIO, he became the new organization's vice president. *Photo reproduced by permission of the Corbis Corporation.*

Thomas J. Watson Jr. (1914–1993) In 1952, Thomas J. Watson Jr. succeeded his father as the president of IBM. At the time, the company was a leading producer of office equipment; IBM had not entered the computer field because the senior Watson did not foresee a future for machines that specialized in data processing. Unlike his father, Watson Jr. understood that computers, if properly marketed, soon might dominate the business world. Under his leadership, within five years, IBM became responsible for over half the computers sold in the United States. *Photo reproduced by permission of AP/Wide World Photos.*

Charles E. Wilson (1890–1961) Charles E. Wilson is best remembered for a legendary declaration that he actually did not make: "What's good for General Motors is good for the country." Nonetheless, he was a major player at General Motors (GM), America's leading automobile manufacturer and the world's largest corporation. As GM's CEO, Wilson successfully negotiated labor agreements with the United Auto Workers, granting employees pension plans and salary increases that matched the rising cost of living. Wilson also served as secretary of defense under President Dwight Eisenhower. *Photo reproduced courtesy of the Library of Congress.*

❖ ADVERTISING

The rise in popularity of television during the 1950s afforded manufacturers a new and powerful outlet through which to advertise their products. This was the precable television era, when all one had to do to view all available TV programs was purchase a set. Even though noncable (or network) television has come to be known as "free TV," its viewers have always paid a hidden price. That price: being bombarded by the television advertising that interrupts the TV series, movies, or sporting events they are watching.

During the decade, products often were incorporated into television series names. Typical examples included *Schlitz Playhouse of Stars* (1951–59); *Philco TV Playhouse* (1948–55); *General Electric Theater* (1953–62); *Lux Video Theatre* (1950–57); and *Chevrolet on Broadway* (1956). The first official name of the comedy-variety show presided over by television pioneer Milton Berle (1908–2002) was *The Texaco Star Theater* (1948–53); after a switch in sponsors, it became the *Buick-Berle Show* (1953). Television stars regularly hyped their show's advertisers on the air. For example, Lucille Ball (1911–1989) and Desi Arnaz (1917–1986), stars of the hit comedy *I Love Lucy* (1951–57), extolled the virtues of Philip Morris cigarettes. (Cigarette advertising was allowed on television until early in 1971.) Years before becoming governor of California and president of the United States, Ronald Reagan (1911–) pitched products on *General Electric Theater.*

To hawk their wares, advertisers reportedly were spending approximately $53 per year for each man, woman, and child in America by 1955; annual spending on marketing doubled during the decade, from $5.7 billion in 1950 to almost $12 billion in 1960. All this nonstop huckstering resulted in a backlash. In mid-decade, *Christianity and Crisis,* a religious-oriented magazine, complained about the pressure being exerted on Americans to "consume, consume, and consume, whether we need or even desire the products almost forced upon us." In his controversial, best-selling book *The Hidden Persuaders* (1957), sociologist and consumer culture critic Vance Packard (1914–1996) offered insight into the manner in which advertisers target markets and convince consumers to purchase their products. Packard observed that different brands of a specific product essentially are the same and that consumers have little reason to prefer one brand of detergent or peanut butter over another. However, advertisers were consulting motivational researchers, sociologists, psychologists,

. . . .

Prior to the television age, magazine advertising often featured movie stars or athletes as pitch-people. In more recent times, companies pay to have their products placed in movies. The idea is that if characters played by Tom Cruise (1962–) or Julia Roberts (1967–) are shown using a particular product, sales of that specific brand will increase.

and other experts in human behavior to detect hidden sources of attraction that might be exploited. If a product could be psychologically linked to winning popularity or attaining love and happiness, sales of that item would skyrocket. On the recommendation of these researchers, companies redesigned packaging to consider the impact of color and artwork on the potential purchaser. In *The Hidden Persuaders,* Packard quoted one advertising executive who remarked, "The cosmetic manufacturers are not selling lanolin, they are selling hope.... We no longer buy oranges, we buy vitality. We do not just buy an auto, we buy prestige."

Sponsors also wielded influence over programming content. On *Man Against Crime* (1949–54; 1956), a detective drama, the sponsor, Camel Tobacco Company, dictated that no villain could be depicted smoking a cigarette. The tobacco firm also made the crime of arson taboo, because lit cigarettes occasionally caused deadly fires. In 1953, writer Reginald Rose (1921–) suggested to the management of *Studio One* (1948–58), a popular CBS dramatic anthology series, produced a teleplay involving racial prejudice in an upscale Illinois suburb. "Thunder on Sycamore Street" as written by Rose depicted a black family who moves into a community, only to have its residents attempt to drive them away. The network and program sponsors, however, asked Rose to rewrite the show to avoid antagonizing Southern audiences. Rose had no choice but to comply, replacing the black family with a character who is an ex-convict.

❖ THE AFL-CIO AND THE TURBULENT TEAMSTERS

The AFL-CIO became one of the largest, most influential labor unions during the 1950s. The American Federation of Labor (AFL), one of the most historically important American labor unions, came into existence in 1886, emerging from the restructured Federation of Organized Trade and

Labor Unions. Originally, the AFL represented only craft (skilled) workers. However, during the early twentieth century, mass production resulted in an increase in the workforce of unskilled and semiskilled workers. An AFL splinter group, whose members disagreed with the exclusion of such workers, bolted in 1935 and formed the Committee (later Congress) of Industrial Organizations (CIO).

During the 1950s, AFL and CIO leadership acknowledged that they had a great deal in common simply because they represented workers—and that there was strength in numbers. Six days after assuming the AFL presidency in 1952, George Meany (1894–1980) observed, "There's too much effort wasted in competition between unions." In 1955, the AFL and CIO merged, becoming the AFL-CIO. This umbrella organization included more than 120 separate unions and represented approximately fifteen million American workers.

The AFL-CIO Executive Council is made up of a national president, a secretary-treasurer, and various vice presidents. The council follows through on policy decisions that come out of biennial conventions, attended by thousands of member-delegates. The primary purpose of the AFL-CIO is to negotiate with employers for pay raises, shorter working hours, and improved working conditions; each member union conducts its own negotiations with management. The AFL-CIO backs political candidates who are proworker; usually, those candidates are Democrats. Additionally, it coordinates labor support for the issues of the day, from education to social welfare to American foreign policy.

In the 1950s, AFL-CIO president George Meany was a powerful political voice. He was a vocal critic of any threat to liberty, whether from the far left or the far right. He deplored communism, believing that Soviet Russia posed a serious danger to the United States. Yet he equally abhorred the tactics of Republican Senator Joseph McCarthy (1909–1957), who played on public fear regarding communist aggression by claiming that subversives were running the U.S. State Department. Meany also condemned the U.S. government's support of right-wing dictatorships that were anticommunist but that stripped their citizens of human rights.

The leadership of the AFL-CIO was not free of discord, however. For example, Meany and Walter Reuther (1907–1970), CIO head and AFL-CIO vice president, disagreed over U.S. foreign policy in Vietnam. The AFL-CIO also was tainted by the presence of criminal elements. The leadership of several member unions, such as the large and powerful International Brotherhood of Teamsters, the trucking union, thrived on stolen funds and cultivated highly publicized relationships with organized crime. With the AFL-CIO merger came the adoption of a set of guidelines for

OPPOSITE PAGE
Walter Reuther and George Meany at an AFL-CIO convention.
Reproduced by permission of the Corbis Corporation.

union officials, stipulating that all corrupt leaders would be banished from the organization. The AFL-CIO cooperated fully with the U.S. Senate Select Committee on Labor-Management Relations, also known as the McClellan committee (named for its chair, Arkansas Democrat John McClellan [1896–1977]), which in 1957 began investigating labor racketeering (the illegal gain of money through threats to a person or organization). Team-

*Dave Beck, president of
the International
Brotherhood of Teamsters
Union, testifying before
the U.S. Senate.
Reproduced by permission of
the Corbis Corporation.*

sters president Dave Beck (1894–1993) was called before the committee, where he was asked about an interest-free loan of between $300,000 and $400,000, which McClellan believed was a misappropriation of union funds. During the proceedings, Beck took the Fifth Amendment sixty-five times. Afterwards, he came before the AFL-CIO Ethical Practices Committee. His refusal to respond to questioning resulted in his expulsion from the Executive Council, and his union's banishment from the AFL-CIO.

Despite AFL-CIO efforts to police itself, a coalition of congressional Republicans and conservative southern Democrats passed the Labor-

Management Reporting and Disclosure Act of 1959, more commonly known as the Landrum-Griffin Act. While the legislation was devised to eliminate corruption in organized labor, it also placed new restrictions on labor organizing and picketing by striking workers. Predictably, the AFL-CIO strongly opposed the Landrum-Griffin Act.

❖ AIR TRAVEL

Before the 1950s, the long-distance vacation was a luxury, even for those who could afford an expensive leisure trip. A typical New York City dweller, for example, who wished a change of scenery might head off by car or bus to a Catskill Mountains resort, located a couple of hours outside the city, or perhaps travel by train to Florida.

However, during the decade, the commercial aviation industry underwent massive expansion. Passenger airlines adopted technological innovations that had been employed by the military during World War II. In order to compete with the railroad industry, they offered inexpensive "air coach class" tickets. These round-trip fares, often as low as $100, allowed middle-class travelers to fly practically anywhere in the United States. In 1953, TWA initiated nonstop air service between New York and California. That airline also advertised the "fastest trips to Europe," even though its planes still needed to refuel during the journey. In 1957, Pan American Airways added to its fleet the first true transatlantic airliner, capable of flying across the ocean without refueling.

All this growth resulted in an expansion of the nation's airports. Airfields that recently had been handling hundreds of passengers now were overwhelmed by tens of thousands of travelers. Paralleling this passenger crush came longer waiting times and increased air traffic. On September 14, 1954, 300 planes were stacked in holding patterns over New York City. A heavy fog had prevented them from landing on schedule, and all of the aircraft had to wait their turn for runway space. This in-flight traffic jam hampered the travel of 45,000 passengers.

New industry safety regulations were implemented in the 1950s. Many more planes traversed the skies than ever before; the number of commercial aircraft rose from 960 in 1950 to 1,647 in 1959. There was a corresponding increase in airplane crashes. On June 30, 1956, the deadliest air disaster to date occurred when a TWA liner smashed into a United DC-7 over the Grand Canyon, killing 128 people. This tragedy resulted in the federal government ordering all airplanes to be equipped with radar. In 1958, Congress passed the Federal Aviation Act creating the Federal Aviation Administration, an agency which dealt with all issues relating to air safety.

Holiday Inn

The increase in long-distance travel during the 1950s spurred a market for clean, inexpensive lodging, which included such necessities as restaurants and amenities like swimming pools. Tennessee-based architect-builder Kemmons Wilson (1913–) acknowledged this need by creating the Holiday Inn motel chain. Wilson's goal was to offer travelers spacious, family-style accommodations at affordable prices. Not only did his inns feature swimming pools, but he also allowed children to stay at no cost and provided free ice, parking, and cribs for infants. Each room came equipped with air-conditioning and television sets.

The first Holiday Inn opened in 1954, outside Memphis. The hundredth, located in Florida, registered its first guest just five years later. Over the decades, the number of Holiday Inns rose to just under two thousand locations worldwide.

Despite increased waiting times at airports and sensational media coverage of air disasters, air travelers would not be deterred. By 1955, more Americans were flying cross-country than journeying by train. Instead of being bound by car or bus to local resorts, vacationers now could fly to destinations that were far from home. A New Yorker wishing to play slot machines could board an airplane and wind up in Las Vegas, thousands of miles away; at the time, Atlantic City had not yet been established as a gambling mecca, and gambling was against the law in all other states. Meanwhile, Florida-bound vacationers could fly south rather than travel there by train, and be just a few hours (rather than days) away from frolicking on the beach.

❖ ALCOA, ALUMINUM, AND THE END OF A MONOPOLY

For the first four decades of the twentieth century, Alcoa (Aluminum Company of America) monopolized the production of commercial aluminum, a lightweight metal that was an inexpensive alternative to steel. During World War II, however, the company was unable to meet the heightened demand for its product, so the U.S. government encouraged such Alcoa competitors as Kaiser Aluminum and Reynolds Metals to increase production. After the war, the government's War Surplus Properties Board sold its plants to Alcoa's rivals, further leading to the demise of the company's monopoly.

Despite this new competition, Alcoa not only survived but thrived. Its revenues tripled between 1946 and 1958, topping out at $869 million in gross sales and $89.6 million in net income (profit). In 1958, Alcoa had four times the production capacity it had two decades earlier, and even expanded its production into other lightweight metals and construction materials.

By decade's end, Alcoa was producing 853 million short tons of aluminum per year, compared to 701 million tons by Reynolds and 609 million tons by Kaiser. All this output by Alcoa's rivals was made possible not only by government intervention, but by what *Fortune* magazine described as Alcoa's "splendid retreat" from monopoly status. The end of the monopoly had benefited Alcoa and the entire industry.

❖ BANK OF AMERICA AND FINANCIAL EXPANSION

During the 1950s the concept of branch banking, banks with remote offices, or "branches," allowed the appropriately named California-based Bank of America to become the nation's largest banking institution. By 1954, "B of A" (as it was nicknamed) oversaw 534 branch offices, achieving this status via a merger with four of its top eastern rivals (National City Bank, Chase National Bank, First National Bank, and Bank of the Manhattan Company).

At the time, states maintained the authority to allow banks to open branches. Except for California, most states still restricted the practice, and no banks could branch across state lines. One fear some people had about the branch-bank concept was that it might lead to a monopoly, with one company, such as Bank of America, controlling a majority of the nation's money flow. However, one advantage of the concept was that if, for example, one Bank of America branch suffered because of a regional financial crisis, it could be supported with funds from branches situated in communities that were flourishing.

While Bank of America's success resulted in the expansion of branch banking into the South and Southwest, at the close of the decade single-location banks still exceeded the number of branch banks, 13,472 to 10,472. Yet the total number of branch banks was steadily rising, and they eventually overtook their single-site competitors.

Additionally, the 1950s saw an increase in such "non-bank banks" as insurance companies, trust companies (concerns that manage trusts and carry out all banking activities except the issuance of bank notes), and holding companies (corporations that hold the stocks or bonds of other companies). Some of these enterprises purchased banks in a variety of communities, sidestepping laws designed to limit branch banking. All were exempt from the strict federal and state regulation under which banks operated, and

Plastic Money

The first credit card appeared in America in 1950, when Diners' Club of New York issued charge cards for use in restaurants. Eight years later, the American Express Company marketed a card for buying goods and services. In both cases, purchases were to be completely paid off upon receipt of a monthly bill.

In 1959, the Bank of America pioneered the initial national "revolving" credit card when it issued the BankAmericard. Purchases made on "revolving" credit could be paid off over time, with a minimum monthly payment required and the balance appearing on the following month's bill. In 1977, the BankAmericard name was changed to VISA in order to appeal to international consumers.

the manner in which they conducted business threatened the commercial banking establishment. This new competition led the American Banking Association to pressure the federal government into passing the Bank Holding Company Act of 1956. This legislation restrained "non-bank banks" from engaging in certain types of activities, and it prevented them from operating in more than one state, unless permitted by the states involved. Despite the increased competition, banks in general flourished during the 1950s, with assets rising to $282 billion by decade's end.

❖ CREDIT, INFLATION, AND PRICE CONTROLS

Before the 1950s, most consumer purchases were transacted in cash and paid for at the time of purchase. A common practice in the 1950s was "buying on time." A person could pay off large purchases in installments rather than all at once. Americans used time payments mainly for such major acquisitions as cars, refrigerators, ovens, ranges, dishwashers and dryers, and record players. Purchases were paid off in monthly installments with interest.

Buying on credit, coupled with more available jobs, higher wages, and increased consumer spending, resulted in inflation (an increase in currency circulating in the economy, leading to a sharp decrease in its value and a rise in prices). In 1952, the federal government reported that, since the mid-1930s, retail food prices had risen by 235.1 percent; between 1950

Post-World War II abundance led to an increase in the American middle class. A generation of Americans who had suffered through the Great Depression of the 1930s and World War II during the first half of the 1940s now savored the fruits of prosperity. More families could afford to own their own homes, choose the communities in which they lived, purchase cars, and own the latest modern household appliances.

During earlier, leaner times, blue-collar workers labored all their lives without ever moving up the economic ladder. Now, many such wage-earners were unionized. This translated into higher pay, better working conditions, and entry into the middle class. Furthermore, more Americans than ever before were earning college degrees, which gave them fatter paychecks and more career options.

and 1952 alone, they had increased 15 percent. In order to control inflation, the government established price ceilings (maximum prices) for a range of goods. The Federal Reserve Board hiked requirements on bank reserves in an attempt to dampen the banking industry's eagerness to allow consumers to "buy on time." The resulting business expense increase was passed on to borrowers via higher interest rates.

Government-imposed price controls were completely lifted in 1953. A recession (a temporary decrease in business activity) between 1953 and 1954 helped slow the rate of rising prices. For the rest of the decade, prosperity and small price increases ruled the American economy.

❖ THE "MILITARY-INDUSTRIAL COMPLEX"

With the exception of the Korean conflict, the United States was not involved in a shooting war during the 1950s. Nevertheless, tensions with the communist-bloc nations, particularly with the Soviet Union, dictated that the United States maintain a standing, fully equipped military force. Despite this need, defense contractors could not turn profits during peacetime because military purchases generally were too small. In order for them to remain in business, the government supported defense contractors with cash-payment subsidies.

Before leaving office in 1960, President Dwight Eisenhower (1890–1969) cautioned the nation about the growth of this interdependence between business and the military, which he labeled the "Military-Industrial Complex." At its worst, this alliance resulted in allegations that the armed forces and defense contractors were conspiring to pad the Defense Department's budget at the expense of taxpayers. In 1953, a House of Representatives subcommittee ordered the military to discipline those accountable for spending $3 million on "useless" navy forklifts, $45 million for "unsuitable" army overcoats, and $1 million for inessential air force chain-link fences.

Whether or not its purchases were wasteful, the government continued to increase its spending on defense. The decade ended with defense spending at $46.6 billion, a 38-percent increase over 1949.

❖ THE NATIONAL HIGHWAY ACT AND THE AUTO INDUSTRY

During the 1950s, as more Americans purchased automobiles, highways and car culture became an essential element of American society. Cars were a necessity, particularly to the new inhabitants of suburbia, where public mass transportation was haphazard and sometimes nonexistent. For Detroit's automakers, the decade proved to be highly profitable. In 1950, manufacturers produced 6.7 million cars, an increase of 1.4 million over the previous decade. By mid-decade, 70 percent of all American families owned cars; in one year, 7.92 million cars were sold. By 1960, Chevrolet offered forty-six different models, thirty-two types of engines, twenty transmissions, twenty-one colors, and more than four hundred accessories.

The increase in car ownership parallels the development of the American highway system. Despite the increased usage of cars, American roadways remained woefully deficient. Expressways had been constructed only in major cities. Outside the eastern part of the country, four-lane highways were nonexistent. America was a nation of mostly smaller roads, which were unable to support the increasing needs of drivers.

Highway construction was in order and, in 1958, Congress passed the National Highway Act, resulting in the building of a 43,000-mile-long interstate highway system. The new roadways were wider, faster, and safer; cross-country travelers could shave days off their trips, driving from coast to coast in less than a week.

One of the downsides of the interstate system was that such legendary roadways as the 2,400-mile-long Route 66, also known as "America's Highway" and the "Mother Road," which extended from Chicago to Los Angeles, were virtually abandoned in favor of the newer superhighways.

❖ SMALL VERSUS BIG BUSINESS

Today, a shopper who wants to purchase a toy likely will head for the nearest Toys R Us. Hungry Americans looking for a quick bite might choose to dine at McDonald's, Burger King, or Kentucky Fried Chicken. Those who wish to sip coffee and savor a pastry might head to the closest Starbucks.

This was not always the case. Before the 1950s, specialized, individually owned "mom-and-pop" shops dotted America's Main Streets and downtown shopping districts. A woman would purchase a dress in a dress shop. A man would buy a suit in a store called a haberdashery. Casual restaurant meals were consumed in single-owner diners, hamburger joints, or spaghetti houses. Everything from draperies to books to appliances came from specialty shops. Departments stores were found in many downtown shopping districts, especially in larger cities, but even these tended to be one-of-a-kind, family-owned-and-operated enterprises.

All this began to change during the 1950s. Small concerns like McDonald's and Baskin-Robbins Ice Cream franchised themselves, and eventually become high-profile restaurant or ice cream parlor chains. Brand names such as Bic (pens), Gerber (baby food), and Culligan (water

By the mid-1950s, 70 percent of all American families owned cars.
Reproduced by permission of American Automobile Association.

The Sun Belt

The 1950s marked the beginning of the migration of American business from the Northeast to the "Sun Belt," a term referring to the southern third of the nation.

At the dawn of the decade, the Northeast, despite being composed of just 8 percent of the nation's land mass, had 43 percent of the U.S. population and 68 percent of manufacturing-related jobs. "Sun Belt" states were blessed with milder climates, wider and more open spaces, and less-expensive land; plus, many were hostile toward labor unions. This was attractive to large corporations looking for financial relief from the compensation benefits that labor unions had managed to negotiate for their members. The widespread availability of air conditioning also made every-day living more comfortable, allowing for a respite from the South's often sweltering heat.

The defense and technology industries spearheaded the southward migration of American industry. White-collar professionals also abandoned the traditional northern industrial centers to take part in the decade's technology boom in the South. Many types of manufacturing companies that did not depend on existing resources in the North also relocated. Not all Northeastern industry and manufacturing interests headed South, but those that did benefited from lower tax rates and living costs, and Southern antiunion sentiments.

filters and softeners) became synonymous with the products or services they marketed nationwide.

The growth of American suburbia directly led to a decline in traditional downtown shopping districts and the growth of the shopping mall. At the mall, a range of stores could be housed under one roof, simplifying the shopping experience. Free parking lots allowed shoppers to browse without worrying that they had outstayed the time left on their parking meters. And even early malls that were not fully enclosed offered shoppers overhead protection from inclement weather as they strolled from store to store, in full view of that convenient free parking. In 1956, sixteen hundred shopping malls dotted the country. Six hundred of them opened that very year.

Corporations became bigger and more powerful during the 1950s as well. In 1951, American Telephone & Telegraph (AT&T) became the first American corporation to have one million stockholders, and its stock prices steadily rose throughout the decade. General Motors was the world's largest company, while Du Pont employed one-third more chemists than could be found in all of America's universities. Corporations also merged with increasing frequency during the 1950s. Among the decade's most prominent corporate unions: Chase National Bank and the Bank of Manhattan Company became Chase-Manhattan; Remington-Rand and the Sperry Corporation became Sperry Rand; the Kroger Company purchased Childs Food; the Brown Shoe Company merged with the G. R. Kinney Company; and the Nash and Hudson automobile companies first merged, and then were absorbed, by Chrysler.

The vast resources of these larger corporations allowed them to spend money on research that led to some major technological breakthroughs. In 1950, a total of twenty computers could be found in the entire United States; most were part of university or government installations. Their combined value was approximately $1 million. The following year saw the debut of the UNIVAC 1 computer, produced by Remington-Rand. Then IBM began producing and marketing computers, heralding the dawn of the information age. Among entertainment-based corporations, CBS and NBC initiated color television broadcasts, while in the travel sector, various airlines began transporting passengers on jet aircraft.

Blockbuster business deals made headlines. In 1957, the share of the 77-story Chrysler Building owned by real estate developer and planner William Zeckendorf (1905–1976) was sold for $66 million. It was the largest real-estate deal in U.S. history. In some sectors of the economy, the decade of growth and success in the corporate world had a negative effect on small entrepreneurs, many of whom were forced to close up shop.

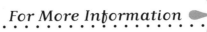

For More Information

BOOKS

Day, Nancy. *Advertising: Information or Manipulation?* Springfield, NJ: Enslow Publishers, 1999.

Feinstein, Stephen. *The 1950s from the Korean War to Elvis.* Berkeley Heights, NJ: Enslow Publishers, 2000.

Gay, Kathlyn. *Who's Running the Nation? How Corporate Power Threatens Democracy.* New York: Franklin Watts, 1998.

Kallen, Stuart A., ed. *Nineteen Fifties.* San Diego: Greenhaven Press, 2000.

Kroc, Ray, with Robert Anderson. *Grinding It Out: The Making of McDonald's.* Chicago: H. Regnery, 1977.

Love, John F. *McDonald's: Behind the Arches.* New York: Bantam Books, 1986.

O'Connell, Arthur J. *American Business in the 20th Century.* San Mateo, CA: Bluewood Books, 1999.

Packard, Vance. *The Hidden Persuaders.* New York: McKay, 1957.

Weiss, Ann E. *Easy Credit.* Brookfield, CT: Twenty-First Century Books, 2000.

Whyte Jr., William H. *The Organization Man.* New York: Simon & Schuster, 1956.

WEB SITES

AFL-CIO Main Page. http://www.aflcio.org/home.htm (accessed on August 9, 2002).

The First Fifty Years of Business Computing Timeline. http://www.cioinsight.com/article2/0,3959,51554,00.asp (accessed on August 9, 2002).

Education

1950: **July 1** The New Orleans Board of Education restores full privileges to married teachers, including the right to promotion (which had not been allowed since the 1930s).

1950: **September 19** African American student Heman Marion Sweatt successfully registers at the University of Texas Law School, where he had been denied admission four years earlier because of his race.

1950: **October 16** The New Jersey Supreme Court upholds the practice of reciting five Old Testament verses each day in all public schools.

1951: **August 18** According to the Associated Press, college costs have increased by 400 percent since the beginning of the twentieth century.

1951: **September 18** Pope Pius XII declares his opposition to sex education in schools.

1952: **March 2** The U.S. Supreme Court rules that "subversives" (those holding communist beliefs) may be barred from teaching.

1952: **April 6** Members of the University of Florida student honor court quit in protest over the reinstatement of two hundred students, including several football players, accused of cheating.

1952: **April 29** With the opening of its coeducational College of Arts and Sciences, the University of Rochester terminates its 107-year-old policy of separate men's and women's colleges.

1953: The Department of Health, Education, and Welfare is created as part of the U.S. president's cabinet.

1953: **February 9** The Phi Delta Theta fraternity at Williams College is suspended for pledging a Jewish student.

1953: **February 11** The National Council for Financial Aid to Education is established to assist colleges in securing funds from business and industry.

1953: **April 3** Fisk University in Nashville, Tennessee, becomes the first historically black college to establish a Phi Beta Kappa chapter.

1953: **June 11** For the first time, the Harvard University Law School awards degrees to women.

1954: **January 7** President Dwight Eisenhower proposes that each state sponsor a conference on education.

1954: **May 17** The landmark *Brown* v. *Board of Education of Topeka, Kansas* Supreme Court decision overrules the "separate but equal" doctrine; segregated public schools are judged to be unconstitutional.

1954: June Attendees at the National Educational Association's national convention vote to sanction school integration, declaring, "All problems of integration...are capable of solution by citizens of intelligence, saneness and reasonableness working together...."

1954: November 19 The U.S. Tax Court declares research and fellowship grants made by philanthropic organizations to be tax exempt.

1955: January 18 The Harvard University Divinity School announces that it will admit women.

1955: May 10 The New York City Board of Education declares that, from now on, students who are two or more grades behind in reading will be held back.

1955: September 2 The U.S. Census Bureau reports that, during their lifetime, male college graduates will earn $100,000 more than their counterparts with high school diplomas.

1955: November 28–December 1 The first White House Conference on Education is held. Its purpose: to study present-day problems in education.

1956: November 26 A Fund for the Republic study determines that blacks show no inherent inferiority to whites in intelligence tests.

1957: September At attempt to integrate Central High School in Little Rock, Arkansas, results in threats, violence, and national headlines.

1957: December 7 American workers average 11.8 years of schooling, with 9 percent finishing college, contrasted to 9.3 years and 6.4 percent in 1940.

1958: March 10 The Vatican Sacred Congregation of Religious Studies sanctions the separation of boys and girls in study halls, sports activities, and classrooms, even in coeducational schools.

1958: September 2 Congress passes the National Defense Education Act.

1958: December 1 Ninety students and three nuns are killed by a fire at Chicago's Our Lady of the Angels school.

1959: October 24 The Department of Health, Education, and Welfare promises to rid the United States of "college-degree mills," alleged institutions of higher learning that grant degrees without requiring academic studies.

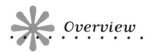

The number-one issue involving education in the United States during the 1950s was school integration. For decades, qualified black Americans had been denied admission to whites-only colleges and public schools. Now, however, black undergraduates and graduate students began petitioning for equal admissions and equal rights.

Additionally, the "separate but equal" doctrine, as outlined by the U.S. Supreme Court in the *Plessy* v. *Ferguson* case of 1896, had long been the basis for segregating whites and blacks in public schools. "Separate but equal" meant that blacks and whites could attend separate schools and thereby receive equal opportunities for education. In reality, however, particularly in the South, the schools attended by white children were more modern and better equipped. In 1954, the Supreme Court, in its landmark *Brown* v. *Board of Education of Topeka, Kansas* case, set aside *Plessy* v. *Ferguson*. The court ruled that "separate but equal" denied black students equal protection under the law. Many states remained determined to maintain segregated school systems, however, and some openly defied *Brown* v. *Board of Education*. These actions resulted in national headlines and, occasionally, in violence.

At the same time that educators celebrated the increasing numbers of adults who were extending their learning experiences beyond high school and college by enrolling in adult-education courses, backers of education lamented the decline in government funding for public schools. As more baby boomers reached school age, they found increasingly inadequate classrooms, teacher shortages, and decreasing school expenditures.

The content of the curriculum in public schools changed dramatically during the decade. At first, progressive-minded educators focused more on a student's emotional, physical, and mental development, at the expense of developing such basic skills as reading, writing, and mathematics. The 1957 launching by the Soviet Union of the *Sputnik* orbiting satellite was a sobering jolt to educators. The *Sputnik* launch was seen as proof that the United States was lagging behind the Soviets in the space race, and educators began refocusing on basic learning skills, especially in math and science.

During the decade, a debate arose that remains hotly contested in the early twenty-first century: Should taxpayer monies earmarked for education also support private and parochial (religion-affiliated) schools? Those who supported the idea of sharing tax revenue among public and nonpublic schools felt that parents who sent their children to private or parochial schools were being unfairly taxed. Their opponents argued that the constitutional concept of the separation of church and state prevented government funding of parochial schools.

At the same time, the "Red Scare" of the 1950s brought the private lives of educators under scrutiny. Politicians wanted to purge schools of anyone with alleged Communist Party ties. Public school teachers and college professors who refused to answer questions about their political beliefs or sign loyalty oaths were suspended or fired from their jobs. Those who condemned such actions argued that academic freedom and constitutional protections were being compromised.

Finally, during the decade, young people increasingly were spending their after-school hours in front of television sets. Educators saw great potential for TV as a learning tool. However, television was born as, and continues to be, a commercial medium. Viewers of all ages were attracted to TV primarily for diversion, so advertising dollars were more available for entertainment programming than for educational purposes.

James B. Conant (1893–1978) Beyond his stature as president of Harvard University, one of America's premier schools of higher learning, James B. Conant achieved fame as an innovative educational theorist. Throughout the 1950s, he called for reform in the American school system. Conant was a proponent of broad curricula for college students, and he urged implementation of a wide range of academic and vocational high school-level courses, to serve all students regardless of their intellectual capabilities. Conant's campaign for higher standards in education culminated in his authorship of *The American High School Today,* published in 1959, which sold a half-million copies. **Photo reproduced by permission of Archive Photos, Inc.**

John Dewey (1859–1952) John Dewey was the founder and president of the American Association of University Professors and the father of "progressive education." Although he lived only two years into the 1950s, his ideas regarding education were at the core of one of the decade's major educational trends. Dewey believed that educators should directly link the learning process to intellectual curiosity and artistic expression, and that students should learn by doing. His critics maintained that students under Dewey's system lacked basic skills.

Orval E. Faubus (1910–) Of all the Southern politicians determined to maintain segregation, Arkansas Governor Orval E. Faubus was one of the most aggressively outspoken. In 1957, Faubus signed four bills into law, each of which impeded school integration. The laws created an anti-integration investigation committee; allowed parents to refuse to enroll their children in integrated schools; required organizations like the National Association for the Advancement of Colored People (NAACP) to reveal membership rolls and financial data; and authorized school district funds to pay for anti-integration legal fees. **Photo reproduced by permission of the Corbis Corporation.**

Theodore S. Geisel (1904–1991) During the 1950s and beyond, Theodore S. Geisel, better known to millions as Dr. Seuss, wrote and illustrated children's books. His stories not only enchanted youngsters but also helped teach them the joys of reading. Among Geisel's books were such verse tales as *Horton Hears a Who* (1954) and the classic *How the Grinch Stole Christmas* (1957). In these rhyming stories, and the countless others he authored over the following decades, Geisel created cleverly rhymed and whimsically illustrated fantasies.

Thurgood Marshall (1908–1993) Thurgood Marshall is best-remembered as the first African American appointed to the U.S. Supreme Court. Prior to his tenure as a Supreme Court justice, Marshall was a civil rights activist. From 1939 to 1961, he worked as a NAACP legal advocate. Among his most famous cases as a lawyer were: *Sweatt* v. *Painter*, argued before the Supreme Court in 1950; and *Brown* v. *Board of Education of Topeka, Kansas,* which came before the court in 1954. Victories in both of these cases helped give black Americans the legal right to educational opportunities equal to those of whites and spearheaded a social revolution in America. **Photograph reproduced by permission of Fisk University Library.**

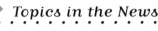

❖ ADULT EDUCATION

Before the 1950s, many Americans had believed that once you dropped out of or graduated from high school, your days as a student had ended. During the decade, however, adults who already had completed their formal schooling began returning to classrooms.

At the dawn of the decade, the average American worker had not graduated from high school. In 1950, just 58.2 percent of all fifth graders went on to receive secondary school diplomas. One of the incentives for adults to continue schooling directly related to salary and quality of life. Educated, skilled workers earned an average of $2,000 more per year than their uneducated, unskilled counterparts, which was quite a large sum at that time. Furthermore, on both a national and global level, a better-educated population would allow the United States to compete in the international marketplace and in the fast-growing world of science and technology.

Federal, state, and local governments began funding educational programs, allowing adults to study agriculture or home economics or to polish their writing and reading skills. To accommodate those in the workforce, classes were held during evenings and on weekends. Appropriations for such classes came mostly from local governments and rose from $129 million in 1950 to $228 million by 1959.

Alongside the trend for formal adult education came an increase in the desire for self-education, particularly among the middle class. In 1947, Robert Maynard Hutchins (1899–1977), former president and then-chancellor of the University of Chicago, founded the Great Books Foundation. Its purpose was to "provide the means of general liberal education to all adults." By 1950, twelve hundred Great Books programs had been started in four hundred cities. Participants read works that the foundation designated as "Great Books" and came together to discuss them in churches, YMCAs, classrooms, and homes. Interestingly, the list included relatively few American authors. It was heavy on ancient Greek and Roman writers and Renaissance European authors.

❖ CHURCH VERSUS STATE

During the 1950s, in a debate that would continue unresolved for decades, government officials, educators, and parents argued the merits of federal funding for private education. In 1950, more than three million students, approximately 10 percent of all youngsters enrolled in American institutions of learning, attended Catholic schools. Many of their parents paid taxes that went toward funding public education. Yet religious schools received no government monies, and parents had to fork out additional sums for tuition fees. On the other hand, opponents of parochial school funding claimed that parents sent their children to such schools by choice, and the concept of separation of church and state prohibited the use of government funds to subsidize parochial schools.

At the time, the movement to win government funding for parochial schools centered on transportation issues. In 1950, Massachusetts Congressman John F. Kennedy (1917–1963) failed in his efforts to convince the House Labor Committee to sanction federal funds for parochial school student bus service. At the state level, Massachusetts governor Paul A. Dever (1903–1958) ignored federal mandates by signing into law a bill allocating federal funds for parochial school busing. On the other side of the issue, the New Mexico state school board banned the transportation of parochial school students in state-owned buses and the distribution of free textbooks to such institutions, while Wisconsin ceased funding fourteen public schools that employed nuns as teachers.

James B. Conant (1893–1978), Harvard University president, added fuel to the debate when he declared that dual school systems, one public and one private, were damaging the American democracy. Conant claimed that the United States could preserve its social continuity only through a single education system. Other related, hotly debated issues included Bible-reading in public schools and the practice of public schools excusing children for one hour per week to attend religion classes.

❖ CURRICULA

To match the rapidly changing times, educational methods and classroom curricula were altered dramatically during the 1950s. Initially, the philosophy of "progressive education" prevailed, emphasizing the individual student's mental, emotional, and physical development, and foregoing the traditional methods of teaching basic reading, writing, and mathematics skills. High schools offered vocational training, plus such electives as photography, botany, and infant care. Modern laboratory equipment and audio-visual aids enhanced the education experience. At the college level, classes in philosophy became standard requirements for a liberal-arts degree, while science-based graduates decreased in number despite the growing high-tech industries.

Critics felt that these curriculum changes were leading to a "softening" of American education, and they campaigned for a return to emphasis on

Funding the Future Through R&D

In 1950, the National Science Foundation began gathering information on the amount of funding available from various sources for use in scientific research and development (R&D). It eventually reported that $334 million had been spent on university campuses during 1953; however, the total national disbursement was $5.2 billion. By 1960, these figures had increased to $825 million and $13.7 billion respectively.

Despite this expansion, the percentage of funds contributed to colleges by industry (as opposed to government) was diminishing. Although scientists and mathematicians trained by universities were finding jobs in the business sector after graduation, they were not funneling money back to their alma maters.

mathematics and the hard sciences. Novelist William Faulkner (1897–1962), speaking at Princeton University in 1958, declared that schools across the country were being transformed into little more than "babysitting organizations." In an address that same year, Arkansas Senator J. William Fulbright (1905–1995) professed that education should spotlight "the rigorous training of the intellect rather than the gentle cultivation of the personality. Courses in life adjustment and coed cooking will not do the job. Mathematics, languages, the natural sciences, and history must once again become the core of the curriculum." In 1946, Fulbright, a former law professor, sponsored federal legislation to create an international educational exchange program. The program, named in his honor, continues to sponsor the studies of thousands of American students abroad.

Advocates of "progressive education" were not as persuaded by critics as they were by *Sputnik*, a small satellite that circled Earth launched by the Soviet Union in 1957. *Sputnik* convinced Americans that their country had fallen behind the Soviets in the space race. Even more importantly, the belief was that the Soviets had developed the ability to launch nuclear missiles aimed at the United States.

The next year, the United States was caught up in a curriculum-revision movement, stressing back-to-basics instruction in science, mathematics, reading skills, and foreign language study. The National Defense Education Act, passed by Congress in 1958, provided $887 million over four years for

During the 1950s and 1960s, no other civil rights leader in America had the impact and influence of Martin Luther King Jr. (1929–1968). In a 1955 speech, King condemned segregation and analyzed the reasons why his fellow black Americans had settled for the "separate but equal" concept. In the speech, he declared, "Many unconsciously wondered whether they deserved better conditions. Their minds were so conditioned to segregation that they submissively adjusted to things as they were. This is the ultimate tragedy of segregation. It not only harms one physically but injures one spiritually."

education that would help further national security goals. Among its provisions: financial assistance for instruction in science, mathematics, and foreign languages, and grants made available for the study of subjects directly related to national defense.

❖ DESEGREGATING EDUCATION: SEPARATE AND UNEQUAL

For decades, public elementary and secondary schools in many parts of the United States were segregated: black children attended schoolhouses in one part of town, while white students went to other schools elsewhere. Segregationists (those that favored the separation of the races) argued that the separate schools offered similar educational opportunities for all youngsters. *Plessy* v. *Ferguson,* a 1896 U.S. Supreme Court ruling, had determined that "separate but equal" facilities for blacks on board railroad trains were not in violation of the Fourteenth Amendment to the Constitution's "equal protection under the law" clause. The arguments made in *Plessy* v. *Ferguson* also allowed states to operate separate schools as long as they offered students the same services.

In practice, however, the institutions serving white youngsters were far superior. They were newer, they were equipped with more up-to-date textbooks and facilities, and they were staffed with the best teachers. To civil rights advocates, the concept of "separate but equal" was a sham.

First, however, activists tackled the issue of blacks being denied entrance to universities based solely on their skin color. Because of his race, a black man, Heman Marion Sweatt (1912–1982), had been denied admission to the University of Texas Law School in 1946. A legal team from the National Association for the Advancement of Colored People (NAACP), the era's highest-profile civil rights organization, took up Sweatt's cause. The case eventually went to the Supreme Court, which in June 1950 ruled in Sweatt's favor. The ruling led the university to establish a separate law school for blacks, which Sweatt declined to attend. Eventually, the court determined that the university had to admit Sweatt to its main law school. Its rationale: The new school was "not substantially equal to those available to white law students." At the same time, a black doctoral student was admitted to Oklahoma State University but was forced to sit isolated from his fellow students in classrooms, cafeterias, and libraries. The Supreme Court ruled that he must "receive the same treatment at the hands of the state as students of other races."

The individuals who worked to change the system were met with a fierce, determined resistance. Despite being ordered by the courts to admit black students, the University of Virginia, University of Tennessee, and University of North Carolina refused to do so. Pronounced Georgia governor Herman Talmadge (1913–), "As long as I am governor, Negroes will not be admitted to white schools." South Carolina governor James F. Byrnes (1879–1972) declared that he would "reluctantly" close schools before "mixing the races."

While attempting to secure law school admittance, Heman Sweatt (who at the time was working in a post office) was harassed by segregationists. He and his wife received threatening notes and telephone calls. His house was vandalized. His life was threatened. However, on September 19, 1950, Sweatt registered at the school.

❖ DESEGREGATING EDUCATION: *BROWN* V. *BOARD OF EDUCATION OF TOPEKA, KANSAS*

Throughout the 1950s, despite determined opposition from segregationists, the NAACP pushed on with its integration agenda. It quickly focused on primary and secondary schools.

In 1953, school integration cases were pending before the Supreme Court from five municipalities: Clarendon County, South Carolina; Prince Edward County, Virginia; Topeka, Kansas; Wilmington, Delaware; and Washington, D.C. All maintained separate schools for black and white students, using as a rationale the "separate but equal" argument. One of these cases, *Brown* v. *Board of Education of Topeka, Kansas,* eventually came before the court. On May 17, 1954, the court overturned *Plessy* v. *Fergu-*

Attorneys George E. C. Hayes, Thurgood Marshall, and James M. Nabrit, smiling after successfully persuading the Supreme Court that separate schools for black and white children are not equal. Reproduced by permission of AP/Wide World Photos.

son. It determined that separate schools for black and white children were not equal, and that black students were being denied equal protection under the law as guaranteed by the Fourteenth Amendment to the Constitution. Even if school districts could prove that, within their systems, all

Not Just a Southern Issue

Not all of the states that defied *Brown* v. *Board of Education* were located in the South. In 1954, by a two-to-one margin, Michigan voters attempted to thwart integration by approving a state constitutional amendment allowing the abolition of public schools. As late as 1958, New York City schools were accused of segregating black youngsters and discriminating against Puerto Rican and Italian students.

Individuals or organizations supporting the equal rights of all Americans regardless of race, religion, or skin color met with harsh opposition. In 1951, four University of Connecticut fraternities—Lambda Chi Alpha, Sigma Nu, Kappa Sigma, and Sigma Chi—lost their national charters for breaking a ban on racial and religious discrimination.

academic programs, facilities, and teacher qualifications were the same, there still would be a negative effect of segregation on the individual student. Concluded the Court's chief justice, Earl Warren (1891–1974), "The doctrine of 'separate but equal' has no place. Separate educational facilities are inherently unequal. Therefore, we hold that the plaintiffs and others similarly situated…are…deprived of the equal protection of laws guaranteed by the 14th Amendment."

While determining that the "separate but equal" doctrine was unconstitutional, and that schools should be desegregated in a timely manner, the Supreme Court offered no course of action on how this might be accomplished. Instead, the court requested arguments in this regard from both sides of the case. This delay allowed segregationists the time to gather their resources and decide how they could obstruct the progress of school integration.

Several Southern states immediately and openly defied the court decision. For example, in November 1954, voters in Georgia and Louisiana approved measures to continue segregated education. After considering the issues at hand, on May 31, 1955, the Supreme Court ruled that the implementation of desegregation was the responsibility of local school officials and the lower federal courts. No timetable was established; instead, the court implored that a "good faith" effort be made by each state to integrate the nation's public schools.

Instead of complying with the court, individual states continued their anti-integration efforts. In 1956, North Carolina voters approved a plan whereby local officials might close schools to avert integration. To work around the *Brown* v. *Board of Education* decision, Virginia and Florida instituted pupil-assignment systems, whereby black and white students could be separated based on newly defined school-district boundaries.

Violence flared when attempts were made to enroll black youngsters in all-white schools, with individual students coming face to face with harassment. One of the most brutal, and highly publicized, anti-integration incidents took place in Little Rock, Arkansas, in 1957. At the opening of the 1957 and 1958 school year, five Arkansas school districts planned to integrate. Just before the first day of school on September 3, 1957, Arkansas Governor Orval Faubus (1910–), a determined segregationist who believed that *Brown* v. *Board of Education* was illegal, declared that blood might be shed if black students attempted to enroll in Little Rock's Central High School. Faubus's comments led to a local court order that the integration should be canceled; however, a higher court overturned the decree.

On the night before the commencement of classes, Faubus directed the Arkansas National Guard to surround the school. This and subsequent actions led President Dwight Eisenhower (1890–1969) to authorize feder-

Because school integration was a controversial matter, these black Arkansas students were escorted into Little Rock High School by federal troops to ensure their safety.
Reproduced by permission of AP/Wide World Photos.

al troops to insure the safe and peaceful enrollment of nine black students. Meanwhile, Faubus declared on national television that the students were the "cause" of the situation. He urged the use of violence to halt the integration, and declared that President Eisenhower had overextended his authority by intervening in what was a state and local issue. As the children attempted to attend school, they were spat on. Angry mobs yelled disgusting insults at them, including "Niggers go home."

Other anti-integration municipalities conjured up plans to avoid desegregation. By 1958, the city of Norfolk, Virginia, established a private educational system similar to one initiated in Arkansas after the Little Rock crisis. Here, students were enrolled in makeshift schools sponsored by churches and private organizations. That same year, the Supreme Court ruled that states could not employ "evasive schemes" to preserve segregation. Nonetheless, at the close of the 1950s, five states—Alabama, Georgia, Louisiana, Mississippi, and South Carolina—still maintained segregated schools.

The spiraling crisis in Little Rock jolted Americans and rippled across the globe. Segregationists felt that the federal government was oppressing them in a manner reminiscent of the pre-Civil War era, when the North and South had disagreed over the enslavement of blacks. Soviet Russian propaganda declared that the U.S. education system was racist, and that the violence surrounding school integration mirrored the problems of a permissive society.

❖ DRAFTING COLLEGE STUDENTS

Prior to the United States' entry into World War II in 1941, American males were subjected to a draft, in which they were selected to serve in the military. In January 1951, U.S. involvement in the Korean conflict led to an active draft of males enrolled in college. Secretary of Defense George Marshall (1880–1959) announced that students could complete the academic year but must then enlist in the military branch of their choosing or risk being drafted. Marshall's proclamation led to a 50-percent drop in spring semester enrollments, as males were panicked into enlisting in order to maintain their choice of military branch.

Two months later, President Harry S Truman (1884–1972) sanctioned draft deferments for college students who maintained top grades and achieved high scores on aptitude tests. By October 1951, 339,056 students, or 37 percent of all those who had taken the tests, had earned deferments. Various draft boards then griped that they no longer could meet their quotas. Because of illiteracy, quite a few Southern boards suffered the same difficulty. In South Carolina, an astonishing 58 percent of all males aged twenty-five to thirty-five tested as functionally illiterate. Other percentages were equally appalling: Louisiana (48 percent); Mississippi (45 percent); Alabama (43 percent); and Georgia (36 percent).

❖ THE "RED SCARE" IN EDUCATION

During the 1950s, many Americans believed that the very survival of their nation, their Constitution and Bill of Rights, and their democracy was being jeopardized by the Soviet Union and the communist-bloc nations. These fears translated into a "Red Scare": a belief that subversives, known as communists and socialists, were infiltrating American political, cultural, and social institutions. Educators at all levels of society came under special scrutiny because they are empowered to influence young people. Those who believed that communism posed a menace to America felt that educators should be scrutinized for their political beliefs and patriotism.

In early 1950, Earl James McGrath (1902–1993), the U.S. commissioner of education, cautioned against allowing communists to teach in public schools. That same year, the National Education Association prohibited communists from attending its annual convention. Local school districts began requiring employees to sign loyalty oaths in which they declared their allegiance to America and American ideals. Universities purged suspected subversives from their faculties.

Such actions caused tumult within school systems. So many alleged subversives were dismissed from the New York City public school system that a teacher shortage resulted. Additionally, such actions were controversial. In 1950, eight New York City teachers who were alleged to be communists were suspended without pay, even though there was no direct evidence of their disloyalty. Then, they were recommended for dismissal based on the Feinberg Law, a controversial statute that barred communists or suspected communists from teaching school. The New York Court of Appeals upheld the law, and the eight teachers were fired a year later. The rationale of the court was that "school authorities have the right and duty to screen" those who "shape the attitude of young minds toward the society in which they live.… " Also in 1951, twenty-six Philadelphia teachers were suspended after invoking the Fifth Amendment and declining to answer questions about their political affiliations.

The content of educational materials also came under investigation, leading to the censorship of school and library books. In 1951, the New York State Board of Regents sanctioned the examination of textbooks for subversive content. Comparable practices were instituted across the country.

At the university level, academics also were required to sign loyalty oaths. Many complained, noting that such demands infringed on their constitutional rights, not to mention their academic freedom. The loyalty oath question was argued before the Supreme Court in 1952. The court determined that individuals could not be denied employment "solely on the basis of organizational membership, regardless of their knowledge concerning the organization to which they had belonged." This decision resulted in the reinstatement of hundreds of university faculty who had lost their jobs over the loyalty issue. However, the issue remained controversial. In 1953, the American Association of University Professors issued a report stating that Communist Party membership was sufficient grounds to fire a faculty member. Yet the association also condemned loyalty oaths, book banning, and congressional investigations into the political beliefs and activities of American citizens.

❖ SCHOOL SHORTAGES

After World War II, Americans by the millions married and promptly started families. The result was a baby boom, with the children of this generation coming to be known as baby boomers. The number of children attending school had remained virtually unchanged from the 1930s through 1952, which was the first year that baby boomers were enrolled in school. More followed each fall, causing school populations to increase every year by between 1.5 and 2 million. In fact, during the 1950s, the number of elementary school students across the nation expanded by 50 percent.

It was for good reason, then, that educators and school administrators became concerned about an emerging shortage of teachers, classrooms, and school supplies. As early as February 1950, the U.S. Office of Education proclaimed that the country's education system was in disarray. It was estimated that $10 billion would be required to hire more teachers and build or improve schools; the following year, the figure was readjusted to $14 billion. Meanwhile, the office reported that school expenditures were decreasing for municipalities with populations over 2,500. It was a situation that Earl James McGrath (1902–1993), the U.S. commissioner of education, labeled "shocking." McGrath noted that, in 1951, "one out of every five schoolhouses now in use throughout the United States should be abandoned or extensively remodeled because they are fire hazards, obsolete, or health risks." Twenty-five percent of all elementary school students attended schools that lacked indoor bathroom facilities! At mid-decade, 39,061 one-room, single-teacher schoolhouses still existed across the country.

Added to all this were rising concerns over teacher training. In 1951, a commission on teacher education and professional standards, sponsored by the National Educational Association, described education-oriented college training as "chaotic."

In 1950, the U.S. Chamber of Commerce reported that the annual cost of educating a child had risen 37 percent during the previous decade. Including inflation adjustments, the figure had increased from $92 per pupil in 1940 to $232 in 1950; by 1960, it was up to $433. Nonetheless, the percentage of national income devoted to education had decreased between 1940 and 1950, from 15.31 percent to 8.24 percent.

"U.S. education is undoubtedly worse than it was 25 years ago," declared educator Robert Maynard Hutchins (1899–1977) in 1951. "All we can say of American education is that it's a colossal housing project designed to keep young people out of worse places until they are able to go to work."

By 1956, the federal government was allocating just 4.5 percent of the cost of educating a student. The previous year, Earl James McGrath resigned as education commissioner, noting that insufficient government monies allotted for teaching the young "are making it impossible...to serve education in this country through this office."

Local and state governments, already hard-pressed to fund education budgets, began requesting additional federal aid. However, attempts to add provisions to education bills resulted in their defeat. The amendments usually involved the promotion of integration or the funding of parochial schools. One school construction bill was defeated in Congress because of a rider, which called for funding only those states that complied with *Brown v. Board of Education*.

Additional federal monies were allocated for education during the decade, in particular after the Soviet Union's 1957 launching of *Sputnik*. However, the amounts were still insufficient. Too many American schools remained overcrowded and underfunded.

❖ TELEVISION'S EFFECT ON EDUCATION

As more American households purchased television sets in the 1950s, children increasingly spent more time indoors, gazing at the images on their TVs. As early as 1950, a study charted the amount of time students at Burdick Junior High in Stamford, Connecticut, a typical American school, spent watching television. The result: Youngsters watched TV for twenty-seven hours a week, almost the same amount of time they were spending in school.

Without doubt, television did increase the amount of information available to Americans of all ages. Previously, visual records of news events only could be viewed in movie theaters; now, news broadcasts and documentaries were seen at home. At the dawn of the television age, predictions were made regarding the medium's potential use as an educational tool. U.S. Commissioner of Education Earl James McGrath, declared, "Through the use of television, educational institutions will be able to bring the greatest teachers, the finest artists, scientists, and philosophers into schools and homes." During the decade, closed-circuit televisions were used in high schools and universities to present education-oriented programming. Western Reserve became the first university to offer full-credit courses by television. Commercial television stations also began airing educational shows. One favorite was *Ding Dong School* (1952–56; 1959), a series tailored to young children. The host, Frances Horwich (1907–2001), head of the education department at Chicago's Roosevelt College, was better-known to viewers as "Miss Frances."

However, audiences of all ages primarily saw television as a medium for entertainment. This fact is perhaps best-illustrated by the 1956 cancellation of *Ding Dong School*, which had aired on NBC five days per week. It was replaced by *The Price Is Right* (1956–65; 1972–), a game show that continued to be broadcast for decades.

Frances Horwich was the host of Ding Dong School, *a popular educational television show that aired during the 1950s. Reproduced by permission of the Corbis Corporation.*

 For More Information

BOOKS

Fireside, Harvey. *Plessy v. Ferguson: Separate But Equal?* Hillside, NJ: Enslow Publishers, 1997.

Fireside, Harvey, and Sarah Betsy Fuller. *Brown v. Board of Education: Equal Schooling for All.* Hillside, NJ: Enslow Publishers, 1994.

Haskins, James. *Separate, but Not Equal: The Dream and the Struggle.* New York: Scholastic, 1998.

Herda, D. J. *Earl Warren: Chief Justice for Social Change.* Springfield, NJ: Enslow Publishers, 1995.

Herda, D. J. *Thurgood Marshall: Civil Rights Champion.* Springfield, NJ: Enslow Publishers, 1995.

Lusane, Clarence. *The Struggle for Equal Education.* New York: Franklin Watts, 1992.

Rasmussen, R. Kent. *Farewell Jim Crow: The Rise and Fall of Segregation in America.* New York: Facts on File, 1997.

Tushnet, Mark V. *Brown v. Board of Education: The Battle for Integration.* New York: Franklin Watts, 1996.

Wormser, Richard. *The Rise and Fall of Jim Crow: The African-American Struggle Against Discrimination, 1865–1954.* New York: Franklin Watts, 1999.

WEB SITES

A Brief History of Distance Education. http://www.seniornet.org/edu/art/history.html (accessed on August 9, 2002).

From Plessy v. Ferguson to Brown v. Board of Education: the Supreme Court Rules on School Desegregation. http://www.yale.edu/ynhti/pubs/A5/wolff.html (accessed on August 9, 2002).

Introduction to the Court Opinion on the Brown v. Board of Education Case. http://usinfo.state.gov/usa/infousa/facts/democrac/36.htm (accessed on August 9, 2002).

chapter four *Government, Politics, and Law*

1950: **February 9** Wisconsin Senator Joseph McCarthy claims to have a list containing 205 known communists employed in the U.S. State Department.

1950: **March 26** A U.S. Senate investigative committee on organized crime opens its nationwide inquiry.

1950: **June 25** North Korean Communist troops cross the 38th parallel into South Korea, resulting in the start of the Korean War.

1950: **November 1** Puerto Rican nationalists attempt to assassinate President Harry Truman.

1951: **February 26** The Twenty-Second Amendment to the Constitution, which limits presidential tenure to two terms, is adopted.

1951: **March 7** General Douglas MacArthur cautions President Truman that a stalemate will develop in Korea unless United Nations troops are allowed to move against China.

1951: **March 22** Alger Hiss, former government official accused of spying for the Soviet Union and convicted of perjury, enters prison.

1951: **April 11** President Truman dismisses MacArthur from his command of the United Nations, Allied, and U.S. forces in the Far East.

1952: **March 29** President Truman announces that he will not be a candidate for reelection.

1952: **November 4** Republican Dwight D. Eisenhower defeats Democrat Adlai Stevenson in the U.S. presidential election.

1952: **November 12** An all-white North Carolina jury convicts a black man of assault for "leering" at a white woman 27 feet away.

1953: **June 19** Julius and Ethel Rosenberg, convicted of passing atomic secrets to the Soviet Union, are electrocuted in Sing Sing prison in New York.

1953: **July 27** An armistice (peace agreement) is signed, ending the Korean War.

1953: **August 25** The American Bar Association approves a resolution to banish communists from the legal profession.

1953: **September 30** Earl Warren is appointed chief justice of the U.S. Supreme Court.

1954: **March 1** Puerto Rican nationalists enter and shoot up the U.S. House of Representatives, wounding five members of Congress.

1954: **April 22** Senator Joseph McCarthy conducts televised hearings on supposed communist infiltration of the U.S. Army.

1954: **May 3** The Supreme Court rules that the systematic exclusion of Mexican Americans from jury duty in Texas violates the Fourteenth Amendment.

1954: **May 17** The landmark *Brown* v. *Board of Education of Topeka, Kansas* Supreme Court decision overrules the "separate but equal" doctrine. As a result, segregated (separated by race) public schools are judged to be unconstitutional.

1954: **June 14** President Eisenhower signs a bill revising the pledge of allegiance to include the words "under God," after "one nation."

1954: **December 2** Joseph McCarthy is condemned by his U.S. Senate colleagues.

1955: **September 24** President Eisenhower suffers a heart attack.

1955: **December 1** Black American seamstress Rosa Parks is arrested for refusing to relinquish her seat on a Montgomery, Alabama, bus to a white passenger. The event sparks a bus boycott by Montgomery's black residents.

1956: **November 6** Dwight Eisenhower is reelected U.S. president. His opponent, again, is Adlai Stevenson.

1957: **May 18–19** President Eisenhower pledges to increase aid to South Vietnam.

1957: **August 29** Congress passes the Civil Rights Act of 1957, which penalizes voting rights violations.

1957: **September 24** President Eisenhower orders U.S. Army paratroopers to prevent interference with efforts to integrate Central High School in Little Rock, Arkansas.

1958: **August 26** The residents of Alaska approve statehood.

1958: **September 4** The U.S. Justice Department uses the 1957 Civil Rights Act to halt alleged violations of African Americans' voting rights in Terrell County, Georgia.

1958: **September 29** Alabama governor James Folsom commutes to life imprisonment the death sentence of a black man convicted of robbing a woman of less than two dollars.

1959: **February 5** President Eisenhower requests that Congress enact a seven-point civil rights program.

1959: **April 23** Soviet premier Nikita Khrushchev rejects Eisenhower's proposals to end nuclear bomb testing.

1959: **August 21** Hawaii becomes America's fiftieth state.

Overview

After the difficult years of World War II (1941–45), Americans settled into what they hoped would be a long lasting peace. Unfortunately, this was not to be. In 1950, just five years after the war's end, the United States found itself involved in another shooting war. This one was in Korea. The U.S. military forces were under the supervision of the United Nations and were pitted against the Communist North Koreans and Chinese. In 1953, an armistice (truce) was signed, with no side designated as victor.

The United States also became locked in a cold war (a war of opposing ideologies) with the Soviet Union during the decade. While no guns were fired, the threat of a confrontation leading to all-out nuclear war remained ever present throughout the decade. This fear was demonstrated in many ways. For one thing, a "Red Scare" swept the country, during which people suspected strangers and neighbors alike of being "subversives," or supporters of communist principles and ideals. At a very public level, this was seen in what became known as the age of McCarthyism. At the start of the decade, Joseph McCarthy, the junior senator from Wisconsin, earned headlines by accusing certain Americans of being communist sympathizers, or Communist Party members. Many of McCarthy's targets were U.S. government employees. Entertainers and other public figures were also suspects. For a time, McCarthy was one of the most powerful and feared men in the country, as he played on the anxieties of Americans regarding the communist threat and inspired others to join him in his campaign to uncover communist sympathizers in every walk of American life. By mid-decade, however, he had been discredited.

Two significant espionage cases dominated the headlines, both of which involved the alleged passing of secrets to the Soviet Union. One focused on Alger Hiss, a former U.S. State Department official. Hiss was accused of stealing government documents, which ended up in the hands of the Soviets. He was convicted of perjury and did time in jail, but maintained his innocence for the rest of his life. The other notorious case centered on Julius and Ethel Rosenberg, a married couple charged with passing atomic secrets to the Soviets. Both were tried and found guilty of espionage. In 1953, they were executed.

In 1957, the Soviets launched *Sputnik,* a satellite, into space. The United States could not ignore the fact that it had been beaten in the race to be the first nation to place a satellite in space. Several questions now gnawed at Americans of all political persuasions. Had the Russians also developed superior nuclear weapons? Would they be willing to use them?

On the national political scene, the Democrats controlled the White House at the beginning of the decade. The president, Harry S Truman, had came into office upon the death of Franklin Roosevelt. Truman won the 1948 election, but chose not to run for reelection four years later. Republican Dwight Eisenhower earned an easy victory in the 1952 presidential race, beating Democrat Adlai Stevenson. The 1956 election saw the same two opponents, and the same results.

Of all the domestic political issues facing the United States during the 1950s, the one that was most far-reaching involved the escalating Civil Rights movement. Until the 1950s, America was almost completely a segregated society. Blacks and whites went to separate schools, ate at different restaurants, and lived in different neighborhoods. However, separate did not necessarily mean equal. The 1954 *Brown* v. *Board of Education of Topeka, Kansas* U.S. Supreme Court decision decreed that separate was unequal with regard to segregated schools. This decision would be a milestone in equal rights for black Americans in all aspects of national life.

Dwight D. Eisenhower (1890–1969) Before becoming the thirty-fourth U.S. president in 1952, Dwight D. Eisenhower had an illustrious career in the military. He was the supreme commander of the Allied troops in Europe during World War II, and he led the D-Day invasion in 1944. Eisenhower, a Republican who was fondly nicknamed "Ike," was reelected in 1956. During and immediately after his years in office, he was viewed as a dull, grandfatherly president who spent the bulk of his time on the golf course. Yet history has most remembered him as a smart, sensible leader with a middle-of-the-road approach to decision making. *Photo reproduced by permission of the Dwight D. Eisenhower Library.*

Estes Kefauver (1903–1963) During the 1950s, Tennessee's Estes Kefauver was a power in Democratic Party politics. Elected to the House of Representatives in 1938 and the Senate a decade later, Kefauver was an unsuccessful candidate for his party's presidential nomination in 1952 and 1956, and its vice-presidential nominee in 1956. He was a political crusader who in 1950–1951 chaired a Senate investigative committee on organized crime. He also was an independent thinker. Kefauver took moderate-to-liberal stances on civil rights issues, which was quite daring for a Southern politician at the time. *Photo reproduced by permission of the Corbis Corporation.*

Joseph R. McCarthy (1909–1957) Wisconsin Senator Joseph R. McCarthy was one of the most controversial figures in American politics, not only of the 1950s but also during the entire twentieth century. McCarthy's defenders viewed him as a patriot who zealously investigated and exposed communists. His detractors blasted him as a shameless publicity-seeker who saw subversives and communists everywhere: in the U.S. Army, for example, or the U.S. State Department. McCarthy's legacy, perhaps, is a term that has entered the American vernacular and that bears his name: "McCarthyism," which stands for the act of charging others with transgressions without offering proof, and accompanied by much publicity. *Photo reproduced by permission of AP/Wide World Photos.*

Rosa Parks (1913–) Rosa Parks is known as the mother of the Civil Rights movement. In 1955, Parks, an African American seamstress, refused to relinquish her seat on a Montgomery, Alabama, bus to a white passenger. She was arrested and fined for disobeying a city ordinance that required her to do so. Parks's bravery and punishment resulted in a boycott of the Montgomery bus line by the city's black residents. The boycott and its aftermath brought to national prominence one of the twentieth-century's preeminent civil rights leaders, Martin Luther King Jr. (1929–1968).

Adlai E. Stevenson (1900–1965) In the 1950s, liberal Democrat Adlai E. Stevenson came into the national spotlight as a successful Illinois governor who attacked the excesses of McCarthyism. In 1952, he was named his party's presidential nominee. Stevenson's campaign was marked by his eloquent speechmaking and insistence on debating the issues, rather than relying on style and image. He lost the election to his Republican rival, Dwight Eisenhower. Stevenson was so admired that the Democrats named him their nominee again four years later. Again, he lost to Eisenhower. In the 1960s, after the Democrats retook the White House, Stevenson served as ambassador to the United Nations. *Photo reproduced courtesy of the Library of Congress.*

Robert A. Taft (1889–1953) The eldest son of President William Howard Taft, Ohio's Robert A. Taft was elected to the U.S. Senate in 1938. During the post-World War II era, he emerged as a leader of the Republican Party's conservative wing. Known as "Mr. Republican," Taft was noted for his firm opposition to pro-union legislation and interventionist foreign policy, and for his efforts to lower top tax rates. Despite his immense power, Taft failed in his 1952 bid against Dwight Eisenhower to win his party's presidential nomination. *Photo reproduced by permission of the Corbis Corporation.*

Earl Warren (1891–1974) Under Earl Warren's tenure as the Supreme Court's chief justice, the court practiced "judicial activism" by overruling earlier decisions and thereby greatly expanded the civil and individual rights of Americans. In 1954, Warren's court handed down one of its most famous and significant judgments: the *Brown* v. *Board of Education of Topeka, Kansas* decision, in which school segregation was declared unconstitutional. Before his 1953 Supreme Court appointment, Warren had served as attorney general and governor of California. In 1948, he was the vice-presidential candidate on the losing Republican ticket. He retired in 1969.

◆◆ *Topics in the News*

❖ CIVIL RIGHTS: THE EMMETT TILL CASE

The details surrounding the death of Emmett Till (1941–1955) offer vivid testimony to the racism that still ruled the South, and much of American society, during the 1950s.

Emmett Till's racially charged murder was a rallying cry for the Civil Rights movement.
Reproduced by permission of the Corbis Corporation.

In 1955, Till was a fourteen-year-old African American Chicago native who was visiting relatives in Mississippi. One August evening, he had an unfortunate run-in with the wife of a white grocery store owner. What exactly happened remains unclear. The woman claimed that Till grabbed her and made suggestive remarks. Some witnesses asserted that he just whistled at her, while others noted that Till routinely whistled to hide a speech defect. Several days later, the shopkeeper, his half-brother, and perhaps several others kidnapped Till from his relatives' home. He was severely beaten. His tormentors supposedly were angered to find a photo of a white woman in his wallet. They shot Till and tossed his body into a nearby river.

The shopkeeper and his brother were arrested and charged with murder. Their trial was heavy with racial tension. After deliberating for a little over an hour, an all-male, all-white jury found the defendants not guilty.

Several months later, the facts surrounding Till's death became public knowledge. William Bradford Huie (1910–1986), a white Alabama journalist, offered the defendants $4,000 to disclose what actually happened. They readily agreed, since they already had been acquitted of the crime and could not be retried. Huie's account was published in the January 26, 1956 issue of *Look*, a popular national magazine. In it, the men revealed how they had beaten and murdered Till. In death, Emmett Till became a martyr for the Civil Rights movement.

❖ THE COLD WAR: THE BOMB

Beginning in the mid-1940s, at the end of World War II and continuing for decades, the United States and the Soviet Union (U.S.S.R.) became

D uring the 1950s, public fear about nuclear annihilation resulted in a boom in the construction of bomb shelters: heavily fortified homes away from home, or homes inside homes, in which families could protect themselves in the event of a nuclear attack.

For five thousand dollars, which was quite expensive, you could transform the basement of your house into a spacious, insulated underground suite. These supposedly devastation-free living quarters came complete with all the amenities, including a Geiger counter to detect the presence of radiation.

However, given the reality of what civilization would be like in the wake of a nuclear war, many viewed bomb shelters as little more than "death traps."

locked in a bloodless conflict that came to be known as the cold war. Each side was vying for an edge over the other, which resulted in their stockpiling nuclear weapons and establishing military alliances with countries across the globe. Pitted against each other were the Western-bloc countries, led by the United States, the democratic nations of Western Europe, and Japan; and the East, mostly comprised of nations with communist governments and led by the Soviet Union. China became involved in the cold war in 1949 when the Communists took power, driving the pro-West government to the island of Formosa (Taiwan).

The decision by the United States to drop atomic bombs on Hiroshima and Nagasaki in August 1945 might have ended World War II. However, the existence of such sophisticated and deadly weaponry meant that any potential future warfare might result in the complete destruction of civilization. In 1949, the Soviets exploded their own atomic bomb, ending the U.S. monopoly on nuclear armaments. Both sides then began developing the next generation of atomic weaponry: the more powerful hydrogen bomb. Warfare had taken on a new face. During the 1950s, it seemed that the United States might one day be going to war, and employing nuclear arms, against the Soviets.

In 1957, many Americans reacted with anxiety and dread when the Soviets successfully launched *Sputnik*, the world's first human-made satellite, into orbit. The popular assumption had been that the U.S.S.R. lagged behind the United States technologically, economically, and militarily. Now, one fact was unavoidable: the Soviet Union had beaten the United States into space. At a press conference, President Dwight Eisenhower

declared that *Sputnik* "does not raise my apprehensions, not one iota. I see nothing at this moment, at this stage of development, that is significant in that development as far as security is concerned." However, such words did little to soothe politicians, scientists, and average citizens. All were well aware that a Soviet satellite, which might possibly be armed with nuclear weapons, was flying over American airspace.

❖ THE COLD WAR: KOREA

Although, no world power was compelled to use nuclear firepower during the decade, a shooting war did break out at the beginning of the decade in Korea, a 600-mile-long peninsula in East Asia that is bounded on the north by China and Russia. After World War II, Korea was divided in half, with Russia occupying the north and the United States controlling the south. The division was formalized in 1948. A war began two years later, after North Korea invaded South Korea. Opposing each other were forces representing the United Nations, mostly from the United States and South Korea, and those from North Korea and Communist China. The United States could have employed atomic weaponry to pound the communists. However, such an action might have provoked the Soviet Union, so no nuclear firepower was employed in Korea. In 1953, an armistice, or peace agreement, was signed, with neither side claiming victory.

Before the war began, the entire population of North and South Korea was approximately forty million people. It has been estimated that up to four million Koreans died in the war. Most were North Koreans, and most were civilians. Meanwhile, over thirty-three thousand American soldiers were killed in action and more than ninety-two thousand were wounded. Today, for the most part, the Korea conflict is regarded as a forgotten war.

❖ THE CASE OF ALGER HISS

As the Cold War heated up, a "Red Scare" enveloped the nation as millions of Americans feared that the Soviet Union and the communist-bloc countries were intent on world domination. During this period, a number of otherwise unknown or obscure Americans found themselves in the headlines, accused of unpatriotic acts against their country. One of the most publicized cases involved Alger Hiss (1904–1996), who in the 1940s was a high-level U.S. State Department official. In 1945, Hiss accompanied President Franklin D. Roosevelt (1882–1945) to the Yalta Conference, where the Allied Powers made crucial agreements on their post-World War II policies. Hiss also was involved in setting up the groundwork for the creation of the United Nations. In these capacities, Hiss had access to classified documents pertaining to American national security.

*OPPOSITE PAGE
Four U.S. soldiers in combat during the Korean War.*

After the war, the House Un-American Activities Committee (HUAC) began investigating alleged communist influences in Hollywood and the U.S government. In 1948, Whittaker Chambers (1901–1961), a *Time* magazine editor and former communist, testified before HUAC that, during the previous decade, Hiss had been a Communist Party member. Eventually, Chambers amended his story, alleging that Hiss had given him stolen government documents to pass on to the Soviet Union. Heading the HUAC subcommittee conducting the investigation was Richard Nixon (1913–1994), then a freshman Republican congressman. It was in this capacity that Nixon gained his first national attention.

Hiss was called before HUAC, where he denied Chambers's claims. He also sued Chambers for libel. Nonetheless, Hiss was convicted of two counts of perjury, and spent almost four years in prison. For the rest of his life, he denied his guilt and attempted to win back his reputation. Finally, in the 1990s, Russian historians produced evidence that proved Hiss's innocence; in 1992, a Russian general who had been in charge of Soviet intelligence even stated that Hiss had never been a spy. Others, however, still claim that Hiss was a Soviet operative.

As Hiss was dispatched to a jail cell, Whittaker Chambers authored *Witness,* a best-selling book published in 1952. He also became a respected conservative pundit. Richard Nixon, of course, was elected U.S. vice president in 1952, and president in 1968. While Alger Hiss's innocence or guilt remains a matter of debate, one fact is inarguable: He came to symbolize cold war tensions and anticommunist hysteria.

❖ THE EXECUTION OF JULIUS AND ETHEL ROSENBERG

In the 1930s, Julius (1918–1953) and Ethel (1915–1953) Rosenberg became active members of the Communist Party. After the birth of their first child in 1943, they left the party and embraced a more family-oriented lifestyle.

During World War II, Ethel's brother, David Greenglass (1922–), worked as a machinist at Los Alamos, New Mexico, on the site of the Manhattan Project, the atom bomb research program. In 1950, Greenglass admitted to the Federal Bureau of Investigation (FBI) that he had been involved in a plot to pass atomic secrets to the Soviet Union. He also claimed to have handed over documents to his sister. FBI agents promptly showed up at the Rosenbergs' Brooklyn, New York, home. Within two months, the couple was indicted by a grand jury for conspiracy to commit espionage. At their 1951 trial, no hard evidence against them was offered; however, they were implicated by several of their alleged confederates, including David Greenglass, who agreed to testify in exchange for immunity for his wife.

Throughout the trial, the Rosenbergs maintained their innocence. Yet they and a third defendant, Morton Sobell (1917–), were found guilty. Irving R. Kaufman (1910–1992), the judge on the case, proclaimed that the crime of which they had been convicted was "worse than murder." He condemned Julius and Ethel Rosenberg to die in the electric chair.

For two years, the Rosenbergs appealed their convictions. During this period, their case became international news, with demonstrators protesting the lack of evidence presented during the trial and the severity of the punishment. However, shortly after 8:00 P.M. on June 19, 1953, the Rosenbergs were electrocuted. (Sobell, meanwhile, was sentenced to a thirty-year jail term. He was released from prison in 1969, wrote his autobiography, *On Doing Time* [1974], and maintained his innocence. David Greenglass received a fifteen-year jail term. In the early 1990s, he was known to be living in Queens, New York, under an assumed name.)

Were the Rosenbergs guilty of espionage? Should they have been censured for an even more serious crime: treason? Or were they victimized by the "Red Scare" hysteria of the era and the fact that they once had been Communist Party members? Wherever the truth lies, several facts remain unquestionable: the Rosenbergs were found guilty based solely on circumstantial evidence; and the severity of their sentence reflected the mood of the era rather than the extent of the crime of which they had been convicted. To date, Julius and Ethel Rosenberg remain the lone American citizens ever to be put to death during peacetime for espionage. The Rosenberg case shows the solemn manner in which Americans regarded the two greatest fears of the 1950s: communism and the atom bomb.

❖ THE AGE OF MCCARTHYISM

No single figure is more associated with the "Red Scare" of the 1950s and with exploiting the nation's fears and paranoia than Joseph McCarthy (1909–1957). The junior senator from Wisconsin was elected to office in 1947. Three years later, he informed President Harry S Truman (1884–1972) that the U.S. State Department was filled with employees who were communists or communist sympathizers. In February 1950, he gave a speech in Wheeling, West Virginia, in which he claimed to have in his possession the names of 205 known communists employed in the department. Later, while addressing the Senate, his numbers varied from between 57 and 205 communists. When challenged to offer specific names, McCarthy waffled. He responded that "it would be improper to make the names public until the appropriate Senate committee can meet

"Talking Communism"

One evening in 1950, a year after the communist revolution in China, a Houston, Texas, couple dined in a Chinese restaurant. The woman, a radio writer, asked the restaurant owner several questions relating to a program she was producing on recent developments in China. A man seated nearby overheard the conversation and informed the police that the people were "talking communism." The couple found themselves arrested. They were jailed for fourteen hours before being released.

This was not an isolated incident. By 1957, government agencies had investigated almost six million individuals for alleged disloyalty to the United States, resulting in only a handful of dubious convictions.

in executive session and get them.... If we should label one man a communist when he is not a communist, I think it would be too bad."

Those who viewed McCarthy's tactics with suspicion felt that he was merely a self-promoter who was all too eager to revel in the publicity that came with his allegations. The senator survived his critics, however, and emerged as one of the most powerful and feared men in the United States. He played into the anxieties of Americans with regard to communist aggression, and few of his fellow politicians were inclined to denounce him. Before 1950, McCarthy had been an obscure senator whose political future was in doubt. Now, he became chairman of the Senate's Committee on Government Operations, charged with investigating petty violations within the federal government. McCarthy named himself head of the Permanent Investigations Subcommittee. Then he commenced a full-scale inquiry into alleged communist infiltration of the U.S. Army Signal Corps at Fort Monmouth, New Jersey. In 1954, McCarthy conducted a televised investigation, which came to be known as the Army-McCarthy Hearings. McCarthy clashed on camera with Joseph Welch (1890–1960), the U.S. Army's counsel. At one point, the senator attacked a member of Welch's law firm, leading to Welch's famous rebuke: "Let us not assassinate this lad further, Senator. You've done enough. Have you no sense of decency, sir? At long last, have you no sense of decency?"

McCarthy's televised antics turned the wave of public opinion against him. By the end of the year, he was condemned by his colleagues for "conduct unbecoming a member of the United States Senate." No longer was he portrayed as a staunch protector of American democracy: he had been unmasked as a witch-hunter and a destroyer of the reputations of hundreds of individuals. McCarthy's influence diminished. Three years after the Army-McCarthy Hearings, Joseph McCarthy died of complications associated with alcoholism.

❖ CRIME AND PUNISHMENT

On the night of January 7, 1950, seven masked gunmen broke into the Boston offices of the Brink's armored car company. They tied up the guards and walked off with almost $2.8 million in cash, checks, and money orders. It was the largest amount stolen in a single robbery to date. The FBI labeled the holdup the "crime of the century" and solved it just eleven days before the statute of limitations (the date after which the robbers no longer could be prosecuted) ran out.

In November of that year, a small group of Puerto Rican nationalists violently protested the U.S. presence in their native land. Two of them, Oscar Collazo and Griselio Torresola, set out to assassinate President Truman. They almost succeeded. At the time, the White House was being renovated and Truman was residing in nearby Blair House. The would-be assassins entered Blair House and pulled a gun. In the ensuing fracas, Torresola was killed, along with Secret Service agent Leslie I. Coffelt. Collazo was condemned to death, but President Truman commuted his sentence to life imprisonment. He was freed in 1979.

Organized crime was in the headlines, beginning with the 1950 murder of two gangsters in a Kansas City, Missouri, Democratic Party clubhouse. In 1950 and 1951, Tennessee Senator Estes Kefauver (1903–1963) chaired an investigative committee that set out to determine the extent of the power and influence of organized crime. Several underworld characters found themselves in the glare of the national spotlight. Among them: Frank Costello (1891–1973), a mob boss who agreed to testify only on condition that his face not be shown on television. The Kefauver hearings determined that organized crime was dominated by two syndicates, one headquartered in New York and the other based in Chicago.

The decade's other major federal crime investigation was carried out by the Senate Select Committee on Improper Activities in the Labor-Management Field, otherwise known as the McClellan committee. Arkansas Senator John L. McClellan (1896–1977) was the chair, and the committee's purpose was to look into allegations of corruption in the country's labor unions, specifically the International Brotherhood of Teamsters, a trucker's union.

One of the more intriguing of the decade's crime stories involved a thirty-one-year-old man who deposited his wife and two children at Los Angeles Municipal Airport in 1950. They were scheduled to fly to San Diego. In their luggage he packed a homemade time bomb that was set to explode when the plane was airborne. At the airport, he purchased $25,000 worth of life insurance on his family. His scheme was foiled when the suitcase burst into flames while being loaded onto the plane. Later he admitted that he was seeing another woman and paying child support to a third.

As late as the 1950s, some American judges still were employing peculiar methods to determine guilt or innocence and mete out justice. In 1951, a Charleston, South Carolina, magistrate balanced a Bible on the forefingers of a woman charged with theft. He then declared,

By Saint Peter, by Saint Paul
By the grace of God who made us all
If this woman took the money
Let the Bible fall.

The book fell, and, the defendant eventually admitted her guilt.

Tennessee Senator Estes Kefauver chaired an investigative committee that set out to determine the extent of the power and influence of organized crime.
Reproduced by permission of Archive Photos, Inc.

During the 1950s, crime among adolescents rose significantly. In 1953, the FBI noted that, in statistics reported by 1,174 cities, young adults under the age of 18 were responsible for committing 53.6 percent of all car thefts, 49.3 percent of all burglaries, 18 percent of all robberies, and 16.2 percent of all rapes. A new term for troubled, criminally prone youths entered the language: "juvenile delinquents."

Finally, in 1950, the FBI initiated its "Ten Most Wanted" criminals list. It did so after the publication of a news account of the "toughest" criminals presently at large.

❖ NATIONAL POLITICS: ELECTION 1950

During the decade, the 1952 and 1956 presidential elections were the two primary political races. However, a host of major issues, both international and domestic, were in the spotlight during the decade's off-year elections.

The important questions during the 1950 congressional races were inflation (increasing prices) and the Korean War. In the red-baiting spirit of the day, the Republicans characterized their campaign against the Democrats as one of "Liberty against Socialism." They blamed the current president, Democrat Harry S Truman (1884–1972), for "losing China to the communists." Dwight Eisenhower (1890–1969), then viewed as the front-runner for the 1952 Republican presidential nomination, claimed that America was suffering from a "creeping paralysis" resulting from the increased size of the federal government. The Democrats responded that, by criticizing Truman, the Republicans were compromising national security. The Democrats further lambasted the Republicans for ignoring the needs of farmers and schoolchildren by not supporting federal aid to agriculture and education.

The election ended with the Democrats in control of both houses of Congress. However, there were clear indications that the party's authority on the national political scene was loosening.

❖ NATIONAL POLITICS: ELECTION 1952

After spirited and hard-fought conventions, Republican Dwight Eisenhower and Democrat Adlai Stevenson emerged as their party's presidential candidates. (At this time presidential nominees were determined at national conventions rather than in primary elections.) The incumbent chief executive, Harry Truman, chose not to run for reelection. One reason was that his Gallup poll approval ratings had sunk to a dismal 30 percent.

Checkers Speech

During the 1952 election, Richard Nixon, the Republican vice presidential nominee, came under scrutiny for supposedly using an $18,000 campaign contribution for personal use. At stake were his political life and the outcome of the election. In a thirty-minute-long speech, viewed by a then-record 58,000,000 television viewers, Nixon discussed his financial assets and liabilities. In so doing, he portrayed himself as a normal American who had been the victim of a vicious slander.

During the speech, Nixon referred to Checkers, his family's pet dog. In mock seriousness, he explained that the dog had been a present from a Republican supporter. And guess what, Nixon was determined to keep Checkers. Some winced at Nixon's attempt to elicit sympathy, viewing it as corny. Others were struck by the nominee's pluck. After the speech, the Republican National Committee reported that it had received 300,000 letters and telegrams, almost all in support of Nixon.

Candidate Eisenhower promised to balance the budget, end inflation, and end the Korean War, pledges that were very popular among voters. His running mate, Richard Nixon (1913–1994), alleged that the Democrat-controlled government was riddled with present and former communists. In response, Stevenson denounced witch-hunt politics and championed individual civil liberties, a daring stance given that many of his foes equated civil liberties with "commie rights."

Eisenhower's campaign staff craftily employed the new, popular medium of television to sell their candidate. In his campaign ads, Eisenhower delivered fifteen-second sound bites surrounding visuals of a robust and confident-looking nominee. Stevenson, an eloquent orator, despised television. He was not as carefully marketed to the public. In November, Eisenhower and his running mate Nixon coasted to an easy victory.

❖ NATIONAL POLITICS: ELECTION 1954

A flourishing economy and a president whose Gallup poll approval rating hovered around 75 percent resulted in the Republicans taking a four-seat majority in the Senate and strike a balance with the Democrats in the House of Representatives. Republican candidates won voter favor by extolling the virtues of President Eisenhower and hitching the proverbial ride on his coattails, meaning that his popularity helped them win votes. The Korean War was over. The dollar was sound. The budget was in the process of being balanced. Furthermore, the Republicans claimed that the Democrats were soft on communism.

❖ NATIONAL POLITICS: ELECTION 1956

Dwight Eisenhower ran for reelection in 1956. Given his popularity, no one emerged to seriously question his candidacy. However, Eisenhower had come to believe that, if circumstances thrust him into the position, Richard Nixon was too politically immature to handle the presidency. The president urged his vice president to remove himself from the ticket. Eisenhower's special assistant Harold Stassen (1907–2001) even told the press that he was supporting Massachusetts Governor Christian A. Herter (1895–1966) as a Nixon replacement. But a majority of Republicans still favored Nixon, and he remained on the Republican ticket.

Again, Eisenhower's Democratic opponent was Adlai Stevenson, who had won a tough battle against other potential nominees. Among them were Tennessee's Estes Kefauver (1903–1963), Texas's Lyndon Johnson (1908–1973), Missouri's Stuart Symington (1901–1988), and New York's W. Averell Harriman (1891–1986), who was endorsed by former President Truman.

During the campaign, the Democrats attacked the Republicans for promoting racial segregation. They challenged Eisenhower to cease hydrogen bomb testing and called for an end to the military draft. Despite these issues, a Republican victory was pretty much a sure bet. Under Eisenhower, the inflation rate (the annual growth in the prices of goods and services) had been reduced to 1 percent. The middle class continued to expand. The president was as popular as ever; a March Gallup poll gave Eisenhower a 76 percent approval rating. The only concern was the heart attack that the sixty-five-year-old chief executive had suffered in September 1955. Although his doctors described it as "moderate," some Americans questioned Eisenhower's health and his ability to govern.

Nevertheless, on Election Day 1956, the Eisenhower-Nixon ticket again emerged victorious. It won by ten million votes, doubling the margin of victory achieved four years earlier.

❖ NATIONAL POLITICS: ELECTION 1958

In a nonpresidential (off-year) election that clearly mirrored the ups and downs of national party politics, the voters in 1958 handed the Republicans

Government Versus Private Pay Scales

According to a 1955 report published in *U.S. News & World Report*, upper management employees primarily interested in fatter paychecks should not consider government service. Average 1955 salaries for government and corporate positions are compared below.

Government Position	Corporate Position
Cabinet Member: $22,500	Company President: $120,000
Bureau Head: $14,800	Executive Vice President: $80,000
Budget Director: $17,500	Comptroller: $35,000
Division Head: $12,030	Plant Manager: $25,000
Engineer: $9,360	Engineer: $19,600
Junior Engineer: $4,035	Junior Engineer: $4,300
Lawyer: $7,960	Lawyer: $8,700
Payroll Clerk $3,700	Payroll Clerk: $3,200
Typist: $3,175	Typist: $2,912

their worst political defeat in more than a quarter-century. Democrats by the dozens won congressional seats, with Democrats outnumbering Republicans by a two-to-one margin in the Senate and House of Representatives.

The Democratic victories evolved from a national feeling that the country was losing the cold war and the space race, as evidenced by Soviet Russia's 1957 launching of the *Sputnik* satellite. Meanwhile, southern Democrats blamed the Eisenhower administration for forced integration, citing the president's commitment to send federal troops to insure the desegregation of Central High School in Little Rock, Arkansas. A surge in unemployment also hurt the Republicans.

For the first time in his presidency, Eisenhower found himself vulnerable to widespread criticism, and Republicans in general were on the defensive at election time. Ironically, Eisenhower himself emerged from the 1958 elections with a stronger power base. The voting purged his party of many who had opposed his foreign policy initiatives. Despite their differences over integration, Eisenhower had much in common with conservative southern Democrats. Both wanted a balanced federal budget, a decrease in defense spending, and no additional social programs.

BOOKS

Allen, Zita. *Black Women Leaders of the Civil Rights Movement*. Danbury, CT: Franklin Watts, 1996.

Alonso, Karen. *The Alger Hiss Communist Spy Trial: A Headline Court Case*. Berkeley Heights, NJ: Enslow Publishers, 2001.

Archer, Jules. *They Had a Dream: The Civil Rights Struggle from Frederick Douglas to Marcus Garvey to Martin Luther King, Jr. and Malcolm X*. New York: Viking, 1993.

Banfield, Susan. *The Fifteenth Amendment: African-American Men's Right to Vote*. Springfield, NJ: Enslow Publishers, 1998.

Benson, Sonia G. *Korean War: Biographies*. Farmington Hills, MI: U•X•L, 2001.

Brinkley, Douglas. *Rosa Parks*. New York: Viking Press, 2000.

Cohen, Daniel. *Joseph McCarthy: The Misuse of Political Power*. Brookfield, CT: Millbrook Press, 1996.

Deitch, Kenneth M. and JoAnne B. Weisman. *Dwight D. Eisenhower: Man of Many Hats*. Lowell, MA: Discovery Enterprises, 1990.

Dubovoy, Sina. *Civil Rights Leaders*. New York: Facts on File, 1997.

Gaines, Ann Graham. *Douglas MacArthur: Brilliant General, Controversial Leader*. Berkeley Heights, NJ: Enslow Publishers, 2001.

Goldman, Martin S. *Richard M. Nixon: The Complex President*. New York: Facts on File, 1998.

Hay, Jeff, ed. *Richard Nixon*. San Diego: Greenhaven Press, 2001.

Herda, D.J. *Earl Warren: Chief Justice for Social Change*. Springfield, NJ: Enslow Publishers, 1995.

Ingram, Philip. *Russia and the USSR: 1905–1991*. Cambridge, England: Cambridge University Press, 1997.

Judson, Karen. *The Presidency of the United States*. Springfield, NJ: Enslow Publishers, 1996.

Kort, Michael. *China Under Communism*. Brookfield, CT: Millbrook Press, 1994.

Kort, Michael. *The Cold War*. Brookfield, CT: Millbrook Press, 1994.

Kort, Michael. *Russia*. New York: Facts on File, 1995.

Lusane, Clarence. *No Easy Victories: Black Americans and the Vote*. New York: Franklin Watts, 1996.

Monroe, Judy. *The Rosenberg Cold War Spy Trial: A Headline Court Case*. Berkeley Heights, NJ: Enslow Publishers, 2001.

Moss, Francis. *The Rosenberg Espionage Case*. San Diego: Lucent Books, 2000.

Parks, Rosa, with Jim Haskins. *My Story*. New York: Dial Books, 1992.

Rappaport, Doreen. *The Alger Hiss Trial.* New York: HarperCollins, 1993.

Rasmussen, R. Kent. *Farewell Jim Crow: The Rise and Fall of Segregation in America.* New York: Facts on File, 1997.

Schraff, Anne E. *Coretta Scott King: Striving for Civil Rights.* Springfield, NJ: Enslow Publishers, 1997.

Schrecker, Ellen. *The Age of McCarthyism.* Boston: Bedford Books of St. Martin's Press, 1994.

Schuman, Michael. *Martin Luther King, Jr.: Leader for Civil Rights.* Springfield, NJ: Enslow Publishers, 1996.

Scott, Robert A. *Douglas MacArthur and the Century of War.* New York: Facts on File, 1997.

Vernell, Marjorie. *Leaders of Black Civil Rights.* San Diego: Lucent Books, 2000.

Whitfield, Stephen J. *A Death in the Delta: The Story of Emmett Till.* New York: Free Press, 1988; Baltimore, Johns Hopkins University Press, 1991.

Wilson, Camilla. *Rosa Parks: From the Back of the Bus to the Front of a Movement.* New York: Scholastic Paperbacks, 2001.

Winkler, Allan M. *The Cold War: A History in Documents.* New York: Oxford University Children's Books, 2001.

Wormser, Richard. *The Rise & Fall of Jim Crow: The African-American Struggle Against Discrimination, 1865–1954.* New York: Franklin Watts, 1999.

WEB SITES

The American 1950s. http://www.english.upenn.edu/~afilreis/50s/home.html (accessed on August 9, 2002).

Legacy of McCarthyism. http://www.english.upenn.edu/~afilreis/50s/schrecker-legacy.html (accessed on August 9, 2002).

The 1950s. http://www.nikemissile.net/Coldwar/1950s.html (accessed on August 9, 2002).

White House Historical Association—Timeline. http://www.whitehousehistory.org/04_history/subs_timeline/a_presidents/frame_a_1950.html (accessed on August 9, 2002).

Lifestyles and Social Trends

1950: William J. Levitt expands his mass production home-building techniques, allowing him to build identical, boxlike suburban tract houses.

1950: Miss Clairol hair coloring is introduced.

1950: Orlon, a wool-like synthetic fiber, is introduced by E. I. du Pont de Nemours Company.

1950: *Betty Crocker's Picture Cookbook,* based on General Mills' fictitious spokeswoman, is published.

1950: **July 17** A University of Michigan survey shows that almost half of the U.S. population does not read books.

1951: The first all-glass-and-steel apartment building, designed by Ludwig Mies van der Rohe, is completed in Chicago.

1951: The French clothing manufacturer Izod introduces the Lacoste tennis shirt in the United States.

1951: C. A. Swanson and Sons introduce the first frozen dinners.

1952: The McDonald's Golden Arches are designed.

1952: *Amy Vanderbilt's Complete Book of Etiquette* is published.

1952: R. Buckminster Fuller displays his geodesic dome at New York's Museum of Modern Art.

1952: Production of such synthetic yarns as viscose rayon, acetate, and nylon reaches a new high.

1952: Femininity prevails in women's clothing as cinched waistlines, molded bodices, and yards of wide skirts worn over stiff petticoats become stylish.

1952: Four-inch stiletto heels are introduced on women's shoes.

1952: **July 17** The U.S. Air Force reports a wave of Unidentified Flying Object (UFO) sightings.

1953: Plastic women's shoes become popular.

1953: The Kellogg Company introduces Sugar Smacks breakfast cereal, which is 56 percent sugar.

1953: Sara Lee Kitchens begins mass-marketing frozen cakes and pies.

1954: Seamless nylon stockings are introduced.

1954: The rate at which Americans move into mostly suburban single-family homes rises 33 percent over 1953.

1954: **March** The world's largest shopping center, featuring one hundred stores, opens in Detroit.

1954: **October 27** More than two dozen publishers announce the formation of the Comics Code to regulate the content of comic books.

1954: **December 15** The U.S. observes the first Safe Driving Day, sponsored by the Presidential Traffic Safety Commission.

1955: No-iron Dacron fabric is marketed by DuPont.

1955: The Coca-Cola Company officially inaugurates the name "Coke."

1955: **February 19** A U.S. Senate committee investigating juvenile delinquency denounces comic books as offering "short courses in crime."

1955: **July** Disneyland opens in Anaheim, California.

1955: **October** An African American minister becomes pastor at a white Methodist church in Connecticut.

1955: **November 27** Three Catholic women are excommunicated in Louisiana for beating a teacher who instructs African American and white children in the same classroom.

1956: The TWA Terminal at New York's Idlewild (later Kennedy) Airport, designed by Eero Saarinen, opens.

1956: Plastic is used widely in the furniture industry.

1956: **November 11** The U.S. Census Bureau reports that women outnumber men in the U.S. by 1.38 million.

1956: **December 16** In a controversial action, Francis Cardinal Spellman, archbishop of New York, instructs American Catholics not to see the film *Baby Doll* "under pain of sin."

1957: Los Angeles adopts a revised building code that reflects earthquake-stress engineering technology and allows construction of high-rise buildings.

1957: Wham-O Manufacturing introduces the hula hoop and the Frisbee.

1957: A Florida circuit court determines that a Jewish couple can maintain custody of the six-year-old daughter of a Catholic woman.

1957: **May–September** Evangelist Billy Graham holds a series of highly publicized revival meetings in New York's Madison Square Garden.

1958: Pizza Hut opens its first restaurant in Kansas City, Missouri.

1958: **March 24** Elvis Presley is inducted into the U.S. Army.

1959: Supermarkets account for 11 percent of U.S. grocery stores, yet are responsible for 69 percent of the country's food sales.

1959: A number of Protestant churches speak out in favor of using birth control in family planning.

✳ *Overview*

The 1950s was an era of great upheaval in the United States. By the millions, Americans who had just survived two decades of economic depression and war left the cities for the greenery and open spaces of the suburbs. Suburban towns sprang up like crabgrass across the country. With these instant communities came a new American lifestyle that included suburban malls, fast-food restaurants, TV dinners, drive-in movies, and an oversized, gas-guzzling car in every garage.

The decade was a time in which the roles within the "ideal" American family were clearly defined. The father was the breadwinner. Five days a week, fifty weeks a year, he donned his gray flannel suit, hopped into his car or on a commuter train, and headed off to earn money to support his wife, his ever-growing family, and their materialistic lifestyle. Meanwhile, his "little woman" remained home and raised the kids. Life was simple and ordered, and the cornerstone of society was authority. Teachers, police officers, politicians, and clergy were respected, and their pronouncements went unchallenged. Fittingly, most of the decade's architecture and furniture design was spare and functional. (Major exceptions included what came to be known as "Googie" architecture and the style of design labeled "kitsch.") Not surprisingly, femininity reigned in women's clothing styles.

During previous generations, young people had been required to take jobs as soon as they were able, in order to contribute to the family income. Now, their parents indulged them with toys, games, and clothes. Girls collected dolls and stuffed animals, while boys amassed shoeboxes filled with baseball cards. The 1950s, like all other decades, saw its share of fads. In mid-decade, children wore coonskin caps. At the end, they played with hula hoops. When they became adolescents, they bought records; they also sipped malts and downed hamburgers at the local ice cream parlor. Teens and young adults dated, paired off, and "went steady," which were preludes to becoming engaged, marrying, and beginning families of their own.

However, the decade was not without its nonconformity and rebellion. Parents were none too pleased when their adolescent children embraced rock 'n' roll music. Not all teens were clean-cut preppies; greasers sported longish hair and leather jackets and exuded a disdain for authority. On a more telling note, blacks, who had been systematically excluded from the burgeoning middle class, began demanding equal opportunity. But to the majority of Americans in the 1950s, adolescents with attitude and complaining minorities seemed little more than a ripple on the national landscape. There seemed to be no end to the nation's prosperity.

Gabrielle "Coco" Chanel (1883–1971) Gabrielle "Coco" Chanel was one of the most influential fashion designers of the twentieth century. Just after World War I, she designed the first in a series of simple, comfortable dresses and skirts that released women from the era's tight corsets. In 1922, she created her famous Chanel No. 5 perfume. Thirty-two years later, she emerged from a fifteen-year retirement to design a line of clothing that was dubbed the "New Look": casual, shaped women's wear that proved to be immediately popular. *Photo reproduced by permission of Archive Photos, Inc.*

Mamie Doud Eisenhower (1896–1979) Mamie Doud Eisenhower was the perfect first lady for the 1950s. It was a time when home and family were considered to be of paramount importance in American society. During the eight years that her husband, Dwight Eisenhower, was in office, Mamie represented the ideal American wife by radiating quiet strength, supporting her husband unfailingly, and becoming involved in charitable causes. She also found satisfaction in domestic responsibilities. "Ike took care of the office," she explained. "I ran the house." *Photo reproduced by permission of Archive Photos, Inc.*

R. Buckminster Fuller (1895–1983) R. Buckminster Fuller was an inventor, philosopher, mathematician, engineer, architect, cartographer, scientist, environmentalist, poet, author, and educator. One of his many accomplishments was the invention of the geodesic dome, a honey-combed, triangular structure that utilized maximum space while being constructed with a minimum of materials. The domes gained wide acceptance in 1953, after Fuller employed the concept in the design of a 93-foot enclosure for the Ford Motor Company's Dearborn, Michigan, auto plant rotunda. *Photo reproduced by permission of Photo Researchers, Inc.*

John Kenneth Galbraith (1908–) In 1958, John Kenneth Galbraith published *The Affluent Society,* a scholarly book on economics that became a best-seller. In it, he offered a cutting indictment of what America had become: a materialistic society that championed private wealth over public need. As a society becomes more affluent, many unnecessary goods are manufactured, which help maintain the country's high level of production and employment. Demand then follows production, with consumers purchasing goods because they are persuaded to do so by advertising. *Photo reproduced courtesy of the Library of Congress.*

Billy Graham (1918–) During the 1950s, Billy Graham became the world's most famous revivalist. In his "crusades," he eloquently and persuasively preached the tenets of evangelical Christianity. At the core of his preaching was that faith in Jesus brought salvation. He also warned of the dangers that communism presented to Christians and Americans. Late in the decade, he acknowledged the civil rights movement by condemning racism as un-Christian. In 1957, Graham filled New York's Madison Square Garden to capacity with a series of spectacular revival meetings.

Photo reproduced courtesy of the Library of Congress.

Hugh Hefner (1926–) Whether you view him as a liberator or a male chauvinist, one point is undeniable: Hugh Hefner was a purveyor of the concept that the pursuit of pleasure and material gain was the new American way. When *Playboy* magazine, Hefner's brainchild, first hit newsstands in 1953, it represented a new openness about sexuality. *Playboy* combined female nudity with stories and articles penned by the nation's top writers. It was an immediate sensation, partially because Hefner had the foresight to run as the magazine's first centerfold, a nude photo of Marilyn Monroe taken before she became a movie star. *Photo reproduced by permission of Archive Photos, Inc.*

Reinhold Niebuhr (1892–1971) Throughout the 1950s, Protestant theologian Reinhold Niebuhr was an influential figure in American religious thought. In the 1930s, Niebuhr had been a socialist, but by the early 1950s he had returned to traditional Protestant values. In particular, he was concerned with how they related to modern society. Niebuhr emphasized what he believed to be man's sinful nature and distance from God, and the need for the mediating presence of Jesus. *Photo reproduced by permission of the Corbis Corporation.*

Francis Spellman (1889–1967) Francis Spellman was the leading American Roman Catholic clergyman of the mid-twentieth century. He was a controversial figure who readily engaged in public quarrels with those he opposed. They included figures as revered as former First Lady Eleanor Roosevelt, with whom he disagreed over government aid to parochial schools. Two of Spellman's pet concerns were establishing diplomatic relations with Vatican City and motion picture censorship. He often linked his religion with patriotism, and accused his opponents of being anti-Catholic. Meanwhile, his enemies sarcastically dubbed him "the American Pope."

Photo reproduced by permission of the Corbis Corporation.

◆ *Topics in the News* . . . .

❖ ARCHITECTURE

During the 1950s, the United States was the undisputed center of architectural innovation. Great architects such as Frank Lloyd Wright, Walter Gropius, Ludwig Mies van der Rohe, Eero Saarinen, Philip Johnson, and Edward Durrell Stone all were active in America. The quality and output of their work was overwhelming.

Wright and van der Rohe were the two whose work had the greatest lasting influence. Wright was the twentieth-century's leading architect. Even though he already was elderly, and did not live out the decade, Wright created some of his most important works during the 1950s. His Price Tower in Bartlesville, Oklahoma, was a clever variation of a high-rise housing structure. His Solomon R. Guggenheim Museum in New York City was a free-form creation in an urban environment. Of the more than eleven hundred public and residential buildings Wright designed during his career, almost one-third were initiated in the 1950s. Quite a few, including the Grady Gammage Auditorium at Arizona State University and churches near Milwaukee and Madison, Wisconsin, were completed after his death.

Van der Rohe designed functional glass, brick, and steel buildings, with concrete slabs creating the ceilings and floors. One of his more expansive projects was the design of the entire campus complex at the Illinois Institute of Technology in Chicago, completed between 1938 and 1955. Van der Rohe's teaching position at the institute allowed him to directly influence countless future architects.

Additionally, the availability of new construction materials combined with post-World War II optimism to allow designers to create outrageous commercial buildings that seized the attention of the consumer. Detractors dubbed this design style "coffee-shop modern" and the "Googie" school of architecture. This style emerged from California, and was characterized by bright, showy colors, exposed neon tubing, shiny metallic reflections, and glossy interior lighting. It was employed in the design of supermarkets, motels, car washes, bowling alleys, and even homes and churches. The original McDonald's Golden Arch is a classic example of "Googie" architecture.

❖ BLACK CHURCH LEADERS AND CIVIL RIGHTS

At the beginning of the 1950s, American society was divided into black and white. Particularly in the South, the races were segregated through local ordinances known as "Jim Crow" laws. Restaurants and trains, hotels and

Frank Lloyd Wright was an extremely influential architect who designed many important buildings in the United States during the 1950s, including the Price Tower in Bartlesville, Oklahoma.
Reproduced by permission of the Corbis Corporation.

apartment houses, school systems and movie theaters, and even public parks and state voting precincts were designated as being "for whites only" and "for Negroes only." Black Americans could be arrested, fined, and even jailed for trying to eat in a "whites-only" restaurant, or drink from a "whites-only" public water fountain. Meanwhile, during the decade, the vast majority of blacks were shut out of the burgeoning middle class.

Many of the decade's civil rights boycotts originated in black churches, countless movement leaders also were pastors. The Reverend Martin Luther King Jr. (1929–1968), the most celebrated civil rights leader of the 1950s and 60s, was one. After the bombing of his house, King quieted an angry crowd of supporters by declaring, "If I am stopped, our work will not stop, for what we are doing is right. What we are doing is just and God is with us."

*The original McDonald's
Golden Arch is a classic
example of "Googie"
architecture.* **Reproduced by
permission of the
Corbis Corporation.**

❖ CARS

Back in the 1950s, the United States truly became a society on wheels. As Americans by the millions moved to the suburbs, they no longer could depend upon public transportation. Additionally, as they attained affluence, Americans demanded mobility. So owning a car became a necessity, particularly outside the big cities.

By 1954, there were forty-seven million passenger cars in the United States. Eighty percent of American families owned at least one car. Most were American-made, and were long and large. Many featured tail fins, which Cadillac introduced in 1948, and most models were designed for style rather than convenience. Their lengths made them difficult to park, particularly in cities. Their fancy grillwork and chrome trim were a bother to clean. Their gas mileage was abysmal. But they were stylish! Their gleaming exteriors and roomy interiors radiated status and power.

The explosion of cars resulted in the popularity of drive-in movies: outdoor theaters in which moviegoers remained in their cars and watched

During the 1950s, "quick" and "speedy" became bywords in American society. Americans became enamored with fast cars, fast-food restaurants, and even ready-made meals at home. The decade saw the advent of mass-produced frozen food, which allowed busy families to place prepackaged fried chicken, roast beef, or macaroni-and-cheese dinners into their ovens. Then, presto, out would pop a hot meal.

Frozen dinners were no food connoisseur's favorite, but they certainly were convenient. The first ones hit supermarkets in 1951, when Swanson offered a line of beef and chicken pot pies. In 1955, the company marketed "TV Dinners," which consumers ate while watching television. That year, over seventy million TV dinners were sold nationwide.

films projected onto large screens. In 1958, 4,063 drive-in theaters dotted the United States.

The decade also saw the birth and quick demise of the Edsel, a box-shaped car that was advertised as having the perfect design for the growing young family. The first Edsel rolled off the Ford assembly line in 1958. However, by then, those in the car's target market already were switching to smaller, more sleekly designed compacts. The Edsel was discontinued two years later and remains the joke of the automobile industry.

❖ CONFORMITY

Throughout the decade, conformity and obedience to authority were the hallmarks of American society. Americans by the millions entered the middle class, abandoned the inner cities, and settled into newly established suburban communities. In 1950 alone, 1.4 million new housing units were built, mostly in the suburbs. This suburban growth continued through the decade, as an average of three thousand acres of farmland per day was bulldozed into tract housing. If you lived on the East Coast, you might have purchased a mass-produced, boxlike house built by the era's foremost real estate developer, William J. Levitt (1907–1994). Levitt built identical houses, side-by-side, in New York, Pennsylvania, and New Jersey. Communities on New York's Long Island and in Bucks County, Pennsylvania, were even named for him: Levittown. Upon completing construction of his first houses, Levitt included free television sets and washing machines as incentives to prospective home-owners. Eventually, shopping centers were built in the vicinity of these new suburban neighborhoods, consisting of clusters of stores located under one roof and offering plenty of free parking. These malls would be followed by schools, restaurants, libraries, movie theaters, and churches.

In the 1950s, life was ordered. The "nuclear family" was the norm. It consisted of a young husband (who more than likely was a war veteran) and his wife, who had settled into their suburban tract house and had begun to add to the family they had started the previous decade. In 1947, a record 3.8 million American babies had been born. Throughout the 1950s, the U.S. population increased from 150 million to 179 million. By 1958, children fifteen years old and younger constituted almost one-third of the U.S. population.

All Americans, whether from the city, the suburb, or the small town, were expected to look a certain way, act a certain way, and neatly fit into the mainstream. The husbands and fathers were the breadwinners, while the wives and mothers stayed at home, cleaned the houses, cooked the meals, and raised the children. Teens and young adults dated and "went steady," which was a prerequisite to becoming engaged. They were expected to marry, start families, and assume the same domestic roles as their elders.

While the majority of Americans unquestioningly embraced conformity, the decade also saw rumblings among the young and disenfranchised. Adolescents by the millions embraced rock and roll, a raucous and liberating music style. Black Americans began clamoring for equal rights. During the 1960s, these rumblings exploded into a full blown cultural revolution. It was spurred on by the coming of age of the baby boomer generation, many of whose members began questioning everything from racism and sexism in American society to their government's foreign policy.

❖ FASHION AND FEMININITY

In the 1950s, women were supposed to marry and remain at home where they cooked the meals, cleaned the house, and raised the children while their husbands worked. This was a typical and traditional social pattern even before the 1950s. During World War II, however, the role of women in society had changed somewhat. Women had "manned" assembly lines, replacing the men who had turned in their work uniforms for combat fatigues. To support the war effort, some women even entered the military. As a result, women experienced a personal and economic freedom that heretofore had been the exclusive domain of men.

With peacetime came a return to "normalcy" and the expectation that women would cheerfully exchange their paychecks for aprons,

Women's fashions of the
1950s, like this dress
designed by Oleg Cassini,
reinforced the image of
the delicate, feminine
woman. *Reproduced by
permission of the
Corbis Corporation.*

regain their lost "femininity," and return to their traditional roles within the American family. Hairdos and makeup trends, as well as styles in clothing and shoes, reinforced the image of the delicate, feminine woman of the 1950s.

The roles women were expected to assume were depicted in the era's Hollywood movies. Films produced during World War II portrayed women as active participants in the war effort by heroically toiling on assembly lines or in combat situations. Later, after the war and into the 1950s, countless films featured clear messages for women: If you are female and you want to fit into society, your primary role will be that of wife, mother, and feminine object. In these films, professional women were shown to be "unnatural," and unfeminine; usually they were unhappy, as well. Happiness came from turning away from the coldness of the working world to embrace the life of the 1950s' woman at home. In countless postwar films, popular female characters in stressful situations, such as a murder mystery or adventure drama, were depicted as being totally helpless and in need of rescue by a handsome, strong leading man.

This focus on femininity was evident in women's fashions. Christian Dior (1905–1957) was the most influential designer of the decade. In 1947, he introduced a line of dresses that highlighted the natural curves of the female figure. The bosom was emphasized by skintight tailoring; hips were padded; the skirt was mid-calf in length, full, and "extravagant in its use of fabric"; and the waist was slender, or "wasp-like." During the day, women wore pearls. In the evening, they were garbed in full-skirted, sequined gowns. All styles emphasized women's bodies; the "ideal" woman of the decade was shaped much like Marilyn Monroe (1926–1962) or Jane Russell (1921–), two of the decade's top screen goddesses. The so-called ideal was curvier, more full-breasted, and far less angular than the ultra-thin, waiflike "supermodels" who would begin to influence women's fashions just one decade later.

In the 1950s, fur stoles and capes were popular. Handbags and shoes were color-coordinated to match the dress. Hair generally was worn short, and many women colored their hair. Make-up was considered an essential aspect of a woman's appearance, with an emphasis on painted eyes and lips. At the time, Charles Revson (1906–1975), the president of Revlon cosmetics, observed that "most women lead lives of quiet desperation. Cosmetics are a wonderful escape from it—if you play it right."

The few career women during the decade wore woolen suits and neatly ironed blouses. Gloves were imperative, and hats were worn. Some hats were large and showy, but most were small, decorative, and perched neatly on carefully coifed hairstyles.

The Man in the Gray Flannel Suit

During the decade, conventionality was the byword in men's fashions. "Conventionality" was translated into a three-buttoned, single-breasted, gray flannel suit: the uniform of preference for the white-collar business class. This suit was paired with a white cotton shirt, featuring a button-down collar and button cuffs, a trim tie, black leather shoes, and a single-breasted tweed overcoat. Hair was neatly cut. Jewelry consisted of a wristwatch and a wedding band.

When not in the workplace, men dressed more casually and comfortably. In warm weather, Bermuda shorts were popular. Sports jackets, which came in a range of colors and styles, replaced suit jackets. Yet formality still ruled. A jacket and tie were considered appropriate attire for a range of occasions, from dining in a restaurant or attending the theater to going out on a date or even to a baseball game!

As the decade wore on, such cutting-edge designers as Anne Klein, Claire McCardell, Kasper, Rudi Gernreich, and James Galanos established an "American look" by creating comfortable, chic sportswear. Women wore jersey jumpers, tailored slacks, play shorts, Bermuda shorts, house-dresses, and short-sleeved golf dresses during backyard barbecues and weekend car trips, or while watching television or driving the children to school. In any formal situation, a woman never wore slacks. And she only wore dungarees (blue jeans) around the house.

❖ FURNITURE

Most contemporary-style American furniture during the 1950s was spare and lean, without ornamentation of any kind. Designers prided themselves on the uncomplicated, almost stark designs that neatly fit into the new suburban homes that were so different from urban townhouses and apartments. They featured fewer rooms and closets, smaller room sizes, lower ceilings, and double-duty living areas.

Of necessity, a new type of furniture design emerged. It was dubbed American Modern, and was functional, impersonal, and mass-produced, often using such synthetic materials as molded plastic or plywood lami-

Kitsch

During the 1950s, a style of design that came to be known as "kitsch" became popular among the masses. "Kitsch" is a German colloquialism for trash and rubbish. Sneeringly, it has been called the only style ever to have been developed by the middle class. In the future, another word came to be associated with kitsch: tacky.

Examples of 1950s kitsch include lamps whose bases were women's legs, hula dancers, ballerinas, Spanish dancers, or African princesses; clocks shaped like boomerangs, molecules, or balls; ashtrays shaped like boomerangs or amoebas; and sofas consisting of round, soft pillows that resembled oversized marshmallows, attached to a curved iron frame.

nate. Actually, American Modern furniture combined of the principles of German Bauhaus architecture and Scandinavian design (also referred to as the Danish Modern look).

Bauhaus, the most dominant school of architecture and design in the twentieth century, was founded by Walter Gropius (1883–1969) in 1919 at Weimar, Germany. Gropius's teachings were based on the concept of linking form with function. Bauhaus design is ruled by simplicity, and the idea that "less is more." After the Nazis closed the school in 1933, Gropius and many of his teachers settled in the United States. Among Gropius's more influential followers were Ludwig Mies van der Rohe (1886– 1969), who became one of the century's leading architects, and Lyonel Feininger (1871–1956), an artist and caricaturist. Beginning in the late 1940s, such American designers as Charles Eames, Eero Saarinen, Hans and Florence Knoll, Harry Bertoia, and George Nelson combined Bauhaus principles with the simplicity and elegance of Danish Modern to create American Modern.

❖ RESPECT FOR AUTHORITY

During the 1950s, the majority of Americans believed what their political and community leaders told them. Parents admonished children to "respect your elders." Young men in military uniforms were admired. Police officers were community pillars.

Americans like J. Edgar Hoover (1895–1972), the all-powerful director of the Federal Bureau of Investigation (FBI), were deferred to without question, despite the manner in which they had gained and maintained their power bases. At the dawn of the cold war in the late 1940s and early 1950s, Hoover was a major player in guarding the United States against subversion, real or imagined. The bureau's iron-fisted authority was rooted in the files Hoover kept on tens of thousands of Americans who, by Hoover's standards, were disloyal citizens. Often, this information had been gathered by unwarranted or even illegal invasions of privacy.

However, during the decade, Hoover was enormously popular with the American people. Books glorified the FBI, portraying Hoover and his agents as heroic defenders of freedom. One of them, *The FBI Story* (1956), was made into a film, which was released in 1959 and starred Jimmy Stewart (1908–1997), one of the icons of the American cinema.

Hoover response to those who dared to criticize his methods was to target them as disloyal. He viewed the nation's strife over civil rights to be the fault of the liberalism of the Supreme Court. To his way of thinking, civil rights activists were little more than Communist dupes.

In the 1960s, when more citizens—particularly the young—started questioning authority, Hoover began to lose his power. The FBI director had enjoyed a long-established direct channel to the White House. However, new Attorney General Robert Kennedy (1925–1968) tried to curtail Hoover's influence and his active participation in political decision-making. Kennedy also pressured Hoover to hire more black FBI agents. After the assassination of President John F. Kennedy (1917–1963), Hoover's White House link was reestablished. But he had become one more authority figure viewed with derision by younger Americans. Older, more conservative Americans still viewed Hoover as an icon of freedom, law, and order. But, many of their children, and increasing numbers of free-thinking adults, saw him as old, stodgy, and out of touch with modern society. The methods he had employed to maintain his power base and quiet his critics had gone unquestioned in the 1950s. By the 1960s, however, Hoover's tactics were increasingly viewed as infringements on individual civil liberties.

❖ THE SUPREME COURT AND THE FIRST AMENDMENT

The First Amendment to the U.S. Constitution prohibits Congress from passing any law "abridging the freedom of speech, or of the press." Over the years, American courts have ruled that the Constitution's framers did not intend to protect all types of expression. Some forms of verbal, written, or creative expression might be deemed so offensive to society's

Hollywood and Religious Films

The 1950s saw an increase in the number of biblical epics and religious-themed films produced by Hollywood studios. Most were set during the early Christian era. They either were loosely based on fact or were fictional accounts of real events. *Quo Vadis* (1951) involved a romance between a Roman soldier and a Christian. *The Robe* (1953) spotlighted the Roman centurion who had supervised Christ's crucifixion. Its sequel, *Demetrius and the Gladiators* (1954), told the story of Emperor Caligula (12–41) and his search for Christ's magic robe. *The Silver Chalice* (1954) spotlighted the Greek artisan who designed the cup used at the Last Supper. *The Ten Commandments* (1956), a biography of Moses, chronicled the Jews' attempts to seek freedom from their Egyptian slave masters. *Ben-Hur* (1959) followed the plight of Ben-Hur and Messala, boyhood friends-turned-enemies because of their different religions.

tastes that they are worthy of being censored. Critics of these rulings question the manner in which such works have been defined. How does one separate a work that is completely unacceptable from one that is unpopular but tolerable?

During the 1950s, the U.S. Supreme Court rendered several important decisions regarding interpretation of the First Amendment. In 1952, the court struck down the state of New York's ban on *The Miracle* (1948), directed by Roberto Rossellini (1906–1977), a leading Italian filmmaker. The film told the story of a young shepherdess who is impregnated by a hobo whom she believes to be Saint Joseph. The New York Board of Regents declared that the film's American distributor had committed sacrilege by showing it. The case reached the Supreme Court, which ruled that "under the First and Fourteenth Amendments a state may not ban a film on the basis of a censor's conclusion that it is 'sacrilegious'."

In 1957, the Court ruled on *Roth* v. *United States,* a case involving a pornographic bookseller who argued that laws against obscene material violated the First Amendment. In the majority opinion, Justice William Brennan (1906–1997) wrote that "All ideas having even the slightest redeeming social importance...have the full protection of the guarantees [of the First Amendment].... But implicit in the history of the First

Amendment is the rejection of obscenity as utterly without redeeming social importance." However, how does one determine what is obscene? Brennan suggested the following test: "Whether to the average person, applying contemporary community standards, the dominant theme of the material taken as a whole appeals to prurient interests [arouses lust]." This definition raised further questions: Who is the "average person"? How does one define "community"?

Two years later, the Court tested the *Roth* standard. The New York Board of Regents had ruled that a film version of *Lady Chatterley's Lover* (1928), based on the novel by D. H. Lawrence (1885–1930), was immoral because it depicted adultery as a "desirable, acceptable, and proper pattern of behavior." The court unanimously overturned the state's ban.

❖ YOUTH FADS AND FASHIONS: CHILDREN

Before the 1950s, young people had been taught that life was difficult. As soon as they were able, they were expected to take jobs and learn the value of money. However, after almost two decades of depression, war, and sacrifice, America had become an affluent nation. Many parents, wanting childhood to be more pleasant for their children than it had been for them, were quite generous with toys, clothes, comic books, and other material goods. As a result, young people became consumers before they entered the workforce. The television advertising that was fast becoming a constant in their daily lives only reinforced the notion that, as one fifteen-year-old told *Newsweek* magazine in 1957, it is "neat to spend money."

Young children had closets filled with board games, such as "Candyland" to "Go to the Head of the Class." Girls possessed dozens of stuffed animals and dolls. The end of the decade saw the debut of Barbie, a "teenager" doll who came equipped with changeable clothes, jewelry, and purses. Meanwhile, boys owned shoeboxes filled with baseball cards. A pack of cards cost several pennies and came with a stick of gum. Topps was the unrivaled king of the baseball card industry. Boys, and some girls, wore cowboy hats and sported toy guns in holsters. The Western films that their parents had enjoyed in movie theaters decades earlier now made inexpensive television programming, and were adored by youngsters. Additionally, such popular child-oriented television series as *The Lone Ranger* (1949–57), *The Gene Autry Show* (1950–56), *The Range Rider* (1951–53), *The Adventures of Kit Carson* (1951–55), *The Roy Rogers Show* (1951–57), and *Wild Bill Hickok* (1951–58) were all set in the West.

In 1954 and 1955, Fess Parker (1925–) starred as American frontiersman, politician, and folk hero Davy Crockett (1786–1836) on several episodes of the Walt Disney (1901–1966) television series. The segments became astoundingly popular, and it seemed that every child in America sported Davy Crockett T-shirts and replicas of his trademark coonskin cap. "The Ballad of Davy Crockett," the program's theme song, became

In order to create their own sense of community, teenagers employed slang: colorful, descriptive words of their own creation that were not in the dictionary.

Slang phrases and words usually developed regionally. During the 1950s, St. Louis teens called a movie a "hecklthon." A really good film was "real George." In Atlanta, a snob was "pink"; blind dates were called "Joe Roe" and "Joe Doe"; and a failed big-shot was a "hub cap." In Atlanta, something exciting was a "large charge"; friends greeted each other by asking, "What's your tale, nightingale?" and bid farewell with "Black time's here, termite." In Salt Lake City, "she" meant yes and "schnay" meant no. In Boston, scholars were "book gooks"; and a girl who wanted to know the cost of an item would ask, "What's the geetafrate?"

one of the biggest hit records of the era. In the late 1950s, kids were enamored by hula hoops: thin, hollow, circular bands that they spun around their waists while wiggling their hips to prevent the hoop from dropping to the ground. Other popular toys included the Slinky (a wire coil that "walked" down stairs) and Silly Putty (a moldable glob of silicone).

❖ YOUTH FADS AND FASHIONS: TEENAGERS

In 1957, it was estimated that American adolescents spent $9 billion per year. Their purchases included hamburgers and malts at the local ice cream parlor, phonographs, movie tickets, clothes, and records. While their parents preferred popular singers such as Frank Sinatra, Bing Crosby, Dinah Shore, and Perry Como, teenagers listened and danced to rock and roll. Parents preferred the ballroom dancing that was featured on *The Arthur Murray Party* (1950–60), hosted by Kathryn Murray (1906–1999), wife of Arthur Murray (1895–1991), founder of a chain of well-known dancing schools. Teens, on the other hand, favored *American Bandstand* (1957–87), hosted by Dick Clark (1929–), which featured dozens of young people dancing the newest dances and rock and rollers performing their latest hits live.

On the fashion front, young people rejected their parents' styles for their own fashion trends. From the mid-1950s, boys and girls had their

OPPOSITE PAGE
The hula hoop was a national fad during the late 1950s. In 1958 the popular toy sold more than one hundred million units.

own version of the "preppy" look. Preppy boys wore V-neck sweaters, baggy pants, and Top Siders or dirty white bucks. Preppy girls wore sweaters, gray felt poodle skirts, white bobby socks, and saddle shoes. The dirndl dress (sleeveless or with puffed sleeves, and with room for plenty of petticoats underneath) became the first popular fashion designed solely for youth. Boys generally sported crew cuts, while girls wore their hair in short, curly "poodle" cuts or Italian-style shags, or swept it back in ponytails. Preppy boys and girls who "went steady" exchanged ID bracelets or class rings, which girls wore on necklaces. Girls also favored charm bracelets, on which they added ornaments to commemorate each milestone moment in their lives.

The decade's other fashion trend, one that starkly contrasted the "preppy" style, was the "greaser" look. "Greasers" were inspired by the character played by Marlon Brando (1924–) in the 1954 movie *The Wild One:* a surly, motorcycle-riding tough guy with attitude to spare. *The Wild One,* which was banned in Great Britain until the late 1960s, featured a line that became a favorite of greasers and rebels with or without causes. A girl asks Brando's character, "What're you rebelling against, Johnny?" His response: "Whaddya got?"

"Greaser" boys wore tight jeans, leather jackets, boots, and shiny shirts or T-shirts with rolled-up cuffs. Their hair was long, greased with Vaseline, and molded to resemble a duck's tail. "Greaser" girls wore tight sweaters, short skirts and stockings, tons of make-up, and their boyfriends' leather jackets. Needless to say, parents and teachers much preferred the "preppy" look to the "greaser" look.

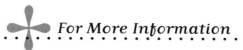

For More Information

BOOKS

Aaseng, Nathan. *More With Less: The Future World of Buckminster Fuller.* Minneapolis, MN: Lerner Publications, 1986.

Baker, Patricia. *Fashions of a Decade: The 1950s.* New York: Facts on File, 1991.

Boulton, Alexander O. *Frank Lloyd Wright, Architect: An Illustrated Biography.* New York: Rizzoli, 1993.

Davis, Frances A. *Frank Lloyd Wright: Maverick Architect.* Minneapolis, MN: Lerner Publications, 1996.

Denenberg, Barry. *The True Story of J. Edgar Hoover and the FBI.* New York: Scholastic Paperbacks, 1995.

Farish, Leah. *The First Amendment: Freedom of Speech, Religion, and the Press.* Springfield, NJ: Enslow Publishers, 1998.

Feinberg, Barbara Silberdick. *America's First Ladies: Changing Expectations.* New York: Franklin Watts, 1998.

Greenberg, Cara. *Mid-Century Modern: Furniture of the 1950s.* New York: Harmony Books, 1995.

Hoag, Edwin and Joy Hoag. *Masters of Modern Architecture: Frank Lloyd Wright, Le Corbusier, Mies van der Rohe, and Walter Gropius.* Indianapolis: Bobbs-Merrill, 1977.

Rubin, Susan Goldman. *Frank Lloyd Wright.* New York: Harry N. Abrams, 1994.

Slocum, Frank. *Topps Baseball Cards: The Complete Picture Collection, a 40-Year History, 1951–1990.* New York, Warner Books, 1990.

Southard, Andy. *Hot Rods and the 1950s.* Osceola, WI: Motorbooks International, 1995.

Southard, Andy and Tony Thacker. *Custom Cars of the 1950s.* Osceola, WI: Motorbooks International, 1993.

Wellman, Sam. *Billy Graham: The Great Evangelist.* Uhrichsville, OH: Barbour & Company, 1996.

Willard, Charlotte. *Frank Lloyd Wright: American Architect.* New York: MacMillan, 1972.

Wooten, Susan McIntosh. *Billy Graham: World-Famous Evangelist.* Berkeley Heights, NJ: Enslow Publishers, 2001.

WEB SITES

The American 1950s. http://www.english.upenn.edu/~afilreis/50s/home.html (accessed on August 9, 2002).

Fashion Flashbacks. http://www.fashion-flashbacks.com/20cen/20cen1950s.html (accessed on August 9, 2002).

1950: Terramycin, a new antibiotic, is developed.

1950: A human aorta transplant is performed.

1950: The hepatitis A virus is isolated and photographed.

1950: Blood tests for tuberculosis are introduced.

1950: Stomach cancers are detected using swallowed radioactive pills.

1950: **February 27** Hilary Koprowski develops the first polio vaccine to be tested on human beings.

1950: **April 18** A patient pronounced dead during surgery is revived through heart massage.

1951: The nausea-inducing drug antabus is marketed as a cure for alcoholism.

1951: Antibiotics are used to stimulate growth in farm animals.

1951: The first full-body X-ray machine is developed.

1951: Leg veins are transplanted to repair faulty arteries.

1951: **September** A report suggests that some cancers may be caused by viruses.

1952: The 190-million-volt deuteron ray combats cancer without breaking the skin.

1952: The polio rate is at an all-time high, with fifty-five thousand Americans stricken by the deadly disease.

1952: **January 30** A patient suffering a heart attack is revived by electric shock.

1952: **March 8** A mechanical heart keeps a patient alive for eighty minutes.

1952: **April 21** Holes in a heart are repaired surgically.

1952: **September 19** The first artificial heart valve is put into a human being.

1952: **November 13** An artificial pacemaker is used to regulate heart rhythm.

1953: A 2-million-volt anticancer X-ray machine is developed.

1953: The first heart-lung machine, which takes over the functions of these vital organs, is used during an operation.

1953: Skin cancer is produced in mice by painting their skins with cigarette tar.

1953: A method for long-term blood preservation is developed.

1953: Psychologists suggest that a sleeping person may learn from a tape recording played within earshot.

1953: **April 11** The U.S. Department of Health, Education, and Welfare is created.

1953: **October 5–9** A human aorta is repaired using animal tissue.

1953: **November 11** The polio virus is first photographed.

1954: Full-scale open-heart surgery is introduced.

1954: **February 23** Mass trials of the polio vaccine developed by Jonas Salk begin.

1955: A surgical procedure for cerebral palsy victims is developed.

1955: The first successful kidney transplant is performed.

1955: **April 12** Salk's polio vaccine is declared a success; large-scale vaccinations begin in the United States.

1956: Research on prison volunteers reveals a cancer-immunity mechanism in human cells.

1956: Researchers find no benefit in the use of citrus fruit extracts high in Vitamin C as cures for the common cold.

1956: The kidney dialysis machine is developed.

1956: **October 15** The existence of an orally administered polio vaccine, developed by Albert Sabin, is announced.

1956: **November 25** The American Cancer Society declares that cigarette smoking and lung cancer clearly are linked.

1957: Synthetic penicillin is developed.

1957: The painkilling drug Darvon is introduced.

1957: A one-minute blood test for the sexually transmitted disease syphilis is introduced.

1957: Synthetic arteries, made of rubberized nylon, are used as surgical replacements.

1958: Athletes' use of drugs to enhance on-field performance is investigated.

1958: A drug is developed to counteract the side effects of penicillin.

1958: The first measles vaccine is tested.

1958: Ultrasound examination of fetuses is introduced.

1958: **October 29** A blind woman reports seeing flashes of light after photocells are implanted in the sight centers of her brain.

1958: **November 18–20** The first National Conference on Air Pollution is held.

1959: The pressure test for glaucoma is developed.

1959: A combined vaccine for whooping cough, diphtheria, and polio is made available.

1959: A resuscitator small enough to be used on infants is developed.

Overview

The 1950s saw great advances in the detection and cure of illness. The breakthrough that received the most publicity involved polio, a dreaded disease that had afflicted President Franklin Roosevelt and was particularly severe when contracted by children. Jonas Salk developed a polio vaccine that was administered by injection. Even though it only was partially effective, it was considered a godsend. As a result, Salk became the decade's most celebrated scientist-researcher. Almost immediately after the Salk vaccine was successfully tested and given to masses of Americans, Albert Sabin announced that he had developed a more advanced vaccine. Not only was this one more effective, but it could also be taken orally. Not long afterwards, polio, a disease whose mere mention resulted in shudders among the general population, was dramatically decreased as a threat to public health.

New surgical procedures revolutionized medicine. For example, heart surgeons could stop the blood flow within the human body, allowing them to repair faulty hearts. For the first time, artificial valves were implanted in hearts, and electric shock waves were employed to control heartbeats. Electric heart pacemakers were also developed to control the pace of the heartbeat. By the end of the decade, open-heart surgery was performed regularly. The success rate of such procedures increased steadily.

Another medical triumph came in 1957, when quick thinking on the part of health care professionals diverted an Asian flu epidemic in the United States through the use of a vaccine. However, not all diseases could be treated, let alone eliminated. While great strides were made in understanding and treating cancer, a cure proved to be elusive. At the same time, a definite and deadly link between cancer and cigarette smoking was established and publicized, much to the dismay of those in the tobacco industry. In response, they had tried to discredit the researchers who connected cigarettes and cancer.

New drugs were developed and introduced to combat a range of diseases. Many of these pharmaceuticals were life-saving additions to existing medical science. Some members of the medical profession were concerned, however, about the over use of other new drugs. In particular, tranquilizers, whose ingredients reduced anxiety and nervous tension, became wildly popular when they were first marketed early in the decade. People craved these "happy pills," and many doctors readily prescribed them. However, others in the medical profession felt that they were being not so much used as abused. Meanwhile, the growth of television as an advertising medium led to an increase in advertising claims by drug makers that the over-the-counter medicines they were marketing cured an assortment of illnesses. Such claims usually were not provable.

Despite all the breakthroughs in disease treatment, one medical specialty remained sorely ignored. Minimal efforts were made to assist the mentally ill, who by the thousands were left to die in understaffed, underfunded facilities. Another subject of concern was the quickly rising cost of health care. Millions were without health insurance; a serious illness that struck an uninsured family could cause financial ruin. Furthermore, what good were all the wonderful advances in medicine if they remained unaffordable? A debate began between those who felt the federal government should take over the health care profession and those who believed it should remain a for-profit business.

Finally, one of the biggest health stories of the decade focused on the September day in 1955 when President Dwight Eisenhower suffered, but survived, a major heart attack.

Thomas A. Dooley (1927–1961) During his service as a U.S. Navy doctor, Thomas A. Dooley treated North Vietnamese refugees. He was deeply affected by their poverty and poor health. After completing military service, he returned to Southeast Asia where he dedicated himself to providing countless individuals with the first medical treatment they ever had received. Dooley was one of the founders of Medico, a nonprofit organization created to help bring medical care to poor regions in Asia, Africa, and South America. Sadly, he died of cancer at age thirty-four. *Photo reproduced by permission of the Corbis Corporation.*

John Franklin Enders (1897–1985) During the late 1940s and 1950s, John Franklin Enders made important contributions to the fight against several infectious diseases. His research, in which he and his colleagues successfully isolated poliovirus, the enterovirus that causes human poliomyelitis (polio), made possible mass production of the vaccine developed by Jonas Salk (1914–1995). Enders' studies resulted in a reduction of the costs incurred by hospitals in isolating and identifying viruses. Enders also worked to isolate the measles virus and to develop a live-virus measles vaccine. *Photo reproduced courtesy of the Library of Congress.*

John H. Gibbon Jr. (1903–1973) In the 1930s, while observing an operation at Massachusetts General Hospital, John H. Gibbon Jr. watched a patient undergoing heart-lung surgery suffocate on his own blood. This experience inspired him to develop an artificial heart-lung device that would allow surgeons to perform delicate procedures that required stopping the heart from beating. The result of Gibbon's research was first used on a human being in 1953, during surgery to close a large opening in the heart wall of an eighteen-year-old female. His heart-lung machine subsequently helped pave the way for modern open-heart surgery. *Photo reproduced by permission of the Corbis Corporation.*

Albert B. Sabin (1906–1993) By the mid-1950s, Americans by the millions were being injected with the Salk vaccine to protect themselves against contracting human poliomyelitis, better known as polio. However, this vaccine was limited in its effectiveness. Albert B. Sabin, who like Jonas Salk was a virologist (a specialist in virus-related diseases), had been researching the poliovirus since 1935. In the mid-1950s, he developed the ultimate polio vaccine. It was taken orally (rather than injected into the bloodstream), and it provided extended immunity from this dreaded disease.

Jonas E. Salk (1914–1995) In the mid-1950s, most every schoolchild knew the name of Jonas E. Salk. That was because Salk had developed the first successful vaccine against polio. Starting in 1955, American children lined up in school to be given the vaccine that would safeguard them against the disease. Even though the Salk vaccine was not 100 percent effective, and was completely replaced within a decade, Americans in the mid-1950s viewed Salk as a hero in the battle against polio.

Helen B. Taussig (1898–1986) Helen B. Taussig was a pioneer in research involving "blue-baby syndrome," a condition in which the narrowness or obstruction of the passages between the lungs and the heart turns the skin of babies blue. In the 1940s, she began exploring ways in which to increase blood flow to the lungs. While doing so, she enlisted the aid of Alfred Blalock, professor of surgery at Johns Hopkins University. Their experiments were successful, but only Blalock earned acclaim. Taussig kept working in relative anonymity for the rest of her career. Historians note that she was understandably bitter at being denied the recognition her male colleague received. *Photo reproduced courtesy of the Library of Congress.*

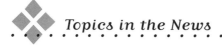

Topics in the News

❖ ASIAN FLU: A CRISIS DIVERTED

In 1918, more people died in a worldwide flu epidemic than had been killed during World War I (1914–18). For this reason, Americans feared a similar catastrophe in 1957 upon the spreading of the Asian flu. Flu (or influenza) is a transmittable disease, caused by a virus, which results in a swelling of the respiratory tract, fever, muscular pain, and intestinal distress. This particular flu was a "Type-A" influenza, the most threatening of all flu viruses. Early in the year, it began appearing in northern China, hence, its name, and it threatened to become the century's deadliest epidemic.

Medical researchers worked quickly to develop a flu vaccine. The vaccine was first tested on fifty-five volunteers at the Maryland State Correctional Institute, and was found to be 70 percent effective. In June, the flu invaded the United States by way of travelers arriving in San Francisco from Asia. By then, many people in the most vulnerable occupations, such as hospital workers, already had been vaccinated. By September, thirty thousand flu cases were reported. However, by mid-month, over eight million doses of the vaccine had been produced. It then was estimated that by the end of the year eighty-five million doses would be available for use: a number that would allow for the vaccination of half the U.S. population. As a result of this thorough preparation on the part of the medical community, America was protected from the Asian flu.

❖ THE BUSINESS OF HEALTH CARE: BILLIONS AND BUREAUCRACY

During the 1950s, great strides were made in medical science with regard to the prevention and cure of disease. Americans were astonished by these accomplishments, but they were also shocked when they learned their cost. Billions of dollars were spent on medical research and health care. Presidents Harry Truman (1884–1972) and Dwight Eisenhower (1890–1969), who, between them, served in the White House from 1945 through 1961, were outspoken supporters of federally sponsored medical research. Under their administrations, government health care and health research-oriented agencies flourished. In 1953, all such agencies were consolidated into the Department of Health, Education, and Welfare.

By 1956, more than $100 million was invested annually in medical research. Yet this remained a modest sum relative to the rise in the price of health care. Six years earlier, total health care costs in the United States were $8.4 million. By the end of the 1950s, they had soared to $17.2 million. Between 1950 and 1957, this rate of growth was 250 percent more than the rise in food costs, 160 percent more than the rise in housing costs, and over 175 percent more than the rise in the total cost of living. In 1959, the average family earned just over $6,600 annually but had medical expenses of $395, or about 6 percent of their income. The standard cost for a hospital room had escalated; the price tag for a day of hospital care was almost $200. Meanwhile, the average doctor earned $16,000 annually, while a surgeon made $25,000.

President Eisenhower warned that, if costs kept escalating, socialized medicine (medical care for everyone, paid for by the government) would result. Those who passionately believed in the private health care system argued that taking the profit out of medicine would remove the incentive for physicians and researchers to continue their good work. Those who supported socialized medicine believed that medical costs were rising at an alarming rate. Poor families were being completely shut out of medical care, and average ones soon would be unable to afford it.

Health insurance promised to insulate individuals and families from the risk of financial ruin due to runaway medical costs, but not everyone could afford coverage. In 1950, approximately one-half of all Americans were covered by health insurance; this percentage rose to 71 percent by the end of the decade. The remaining 29 percent translated into fifty million uninsured Americans. Meanwhile, physicians began to resist the mounting paperwork involved in filing insurance claims. Some busy doctors were forced to hire employees who did nothing but file the various insurance forms.

❖ CANCER: WILL THERE EVER BE A CURE?

Of all diseases, cancer was arguably the most feared during the 1950s. Other maladies, such as heart disease, may have killed more Americans, but a diagnosis of cancer, most commonly defined as malignant (harmful, likely resulting in death) tumors that grow and spread anywhere in the body, was the equivalent of a death sentence.

At the beginning of the decade, some doctors considered cancer to be incurable. Many hospitals even felt it their duty to guard their cancer patients against intrusions by researchers. However, the American Cancer Society and the federal government began devoting enormous energy to fighting the disease, in the belief that researchers one day might uncover a cure. The American Cancer Society's annual budget rose from $4 million in 1947 to $110 million in 1959. In 1953, a cancer research hospital was

Cancer and Smoking

In the 1950s, the most debated cause of cancer was tobacco use. Early in the decade, researchers showed that mice painted with tobacco tars developed skin cancer. Scientists observed that humans who developed respiratory cancer often were smokers. In addition, they pointed out that smoking significantly contributed to the risk of cardiovascular (heart) disease.

America was a nation of smokers. Billions of cigarettes were produced and purchased each year. Cigarette manufacturers and their customers did not want to acknowledge any kind of link between smoking and cancer. In 1954, American cigarette companies formed the Tobacco Industry Research Council, a high-budget, high-profile public relations organization that defended the industry against criticism from health researchers.

opened at the National Institutes of Health complex in Bethesda, Maryland. By that time, health care specialists were more involved in cancer diagnosis. For example, women were advised to visit a gynecologist (a specialist in women's health and diseases), rather than a family doctor, for a Pap smear (a test to identify cervical cancer).

As the decade progressed, three types of cancer cures came to be considered: surgery, in which the malignancy was cut out; radiotherapy, in which the malignant cell growths were subjected to radiation (the process by which energy in the form of heat or light is emitted from molecules and atoms) in an attempt to kill them; and chemotherapy, not yet fully developed during the decade, in which a medicine was taken to attack the malignancy.

As researchers labored to uncover a cure for the disease, alleged quacks and fakers took advantage of desperate cancer patients. One of the most well-known and most controversial of the fakes was Harry M. Hoxsey (1901–1973), who back in 1924 had begun selling pills and liquid medicines that he claimed were miracle cancer cures. Their ingredients included licorice, red clover, and varieties of plant roots and barks. The Food and Drug Administration (FDA) and state and federal courts ruled that Hoxsey's pills were worthless. But to some he was a folk hero, as a succession of his patients swore that his cures worked. By the mid-1950s, Hoxsey was operating seventeen clinics across the country, and he was charging patients $460 per treatment. He kept on offering his pills until his death from pancreatic cancer in 1973.

Hoxsey's methods, however valid or invalid, serve to illustrate the ongoing debate between those who advocate mainstream medical treatment and those who favor the use of herbs and other natural substances to prevent and cure disease.

❖ GERMS: WHAT THEY ARE, AND HOW TO DESTROY THEM

If the general health concerns of Americans during the 1950s could be reduced to a single word, it probably would be germs, or disease-causing microorganisms. However, the average person really did not know much about germs except that they sometimes were passed from one person to another, resulting in the spreading of disease.

The two most feared germs are bacteria (one-celled microorganisms) and viruses (ultramicroscopic or submicroscopic agents). During the decade, researchers made great strides in the understanding and control of these tiny enemies. In 1947, sixty viruses were thought to contribute to human disease; by 1959, seventy-six new ones had been identified. During the 1950s the viruses that cause polio and measles, for example, were actually photographed for the first time. This enabled scientists to learn more about their structure and even manufacture them from materials in their laboratories.

At this time, it was believed that the ultimate remedy for illness lay in shots and pills, particularly those that contained antibiotics (chemical substances, produced by microorganisms, that can stop the growth of or completely destroy bacteria). In 1950, penicillin, the antibiotic fungus discovered by Alexander Fleming (1881–1955) in 1928, was artificially produced for the first time. This breakthrough resulted in the widespread use of penicillin to combat bacterial infections. Other antibiotics were developed during the decade including streptomycin, aureomycin, and neomycin. But as effective as antibiotics were against bacterial diseases, they were powerless against viruses. During the decade, scientists developed vaccines that provided protection against viruses that caused such diseases as polio, measles, and flu, but they could only prevent infection if they were given in advance of the onset. Once an unvaccinated person had contracted a viral disease, vaccines could not minimize the effects of the disease, as antibiotics could with bacterial diseases.

❖ HEART DISEASE: AMAZING NEW TREATMENTS

In the 1950s, half of all deaths in the United States were caused by heart disease: heart-related ailments that at the time were said to include

The President Has a Heart Attack!

. . . .

Americans were never more aware of the perils of heart disease than on September 24, 1955, when President Dwight Eisenhower (1890–1969) suffered a massive heart attack.

He was vacationing in Denver, Colorado, and had put in a full day of golf on the previous day. In the aftermath of the attack, America momentarily panicked. Stock prices plummeted at first, but quickly regained their losses. The president soon recovered, and he returned to the White House on November 11 of that year.

Of his heart attack, Eisenhower later observed, "I had thrust upon me the unpleasant fact that I was indeed a sick man."

over twenty maladies, including arteriosclerosis (hardening of the arteries around the heart) and hypertension (high blood pressure). A major type of heart disease is the inability of vessels to deliver blood to parts of the body. When the defective vessels are in the heart, the result is a heart attack. When they are in the neck or brain, the result is a stroke.

Heart disease became more treatable during the 1950s. Surgeons were performing what seemed like astounding, mind-boggling heart-related surgery. In Philadelphia, an eleven-year-old girl was placed in a freezer to lower her body temperature to eighty-eight degrees, thus allowing doctors to stop her blood flow for five minutes while they closed a hole in the wall of her heart. In Washington, D.C., surgeons implanted an artificial mechanical valve similar to a plumbing device in the heart of a thirty-year-old woman, restoring her to health. By the end of the 1950s, open-heart surgery was being performed regularly. A few years earlier, the success rate of such operations had been approximately 40 percent. The University of Minnesota reported that, at the close of the 1950s, just 2.5 percent of patients died as a result of the surgery.

Electric shock began to be used to control heartbeats and revive lifeless hearts. In 1952, a patient who died during surgery was brought back to life by administering electric shocks to her heart. That same year, the electric heart pacemaker was developed. Initially, pacemakers were about twice the size of a pack of cigarettes. Surgeons placed them under the skin and connected them to the heart by electrical leads. The device put forth controlled electric shocks, which stimulated a regular heartbeat. Batteries had to be changed periodically, but that required only minor surgery.

Some heart-related surgical procedures were still in their exploratory stages. In New York, a flap of skin from the chest wall of a dog was sewn to the surface of his heart so that the blood supply from the skin flap could revitalize a heart crippled by blocked coronary arteries. In Chicago, a healthy heart was transplanted from one dog to another. It kept beating for forty-eight minutes, suggesting to heart specialists that animal hearts might be able to keep humans alive during extensive surgery.

Also during the decade, inroads were made in the area of heart attack prevention. Researchers explored the effects of hypertension (high blood pressure) and levels of cholesterol (a substance found among the fats in the bloodstream and in all of the body's cells) on heart disease. Doctors routinely advised their patients to avoid too much salt, which caused hypertension. High-fat diets also were identified as unhealthy.

❖ "MIRACLE CURES" AND GREED: ANYTHING FOR PROFIT

With the rising popularity of television during the 1950s came an increase in advertising that directly influenced the manner in which consumers chose the products they purchased. It was one thing for advertisers to claim that a certain kind of cereal was tastier, a particular brand of bathroom tissue was fluffier, or a specific toy was more fun than a competitor's plaything. It was quite another to declare that a medicine might cure an ailment when such claims could not be proven scientifically.

As long as products have been advertised, some companies that manufacture them have attempted to make outrageous claims about their effectiveness. In March 1950, the Federal Trade Commission (FTC) charged the makers of the popular medicines Inhiston, Anahist, Resistabs, and Kripton with false advertising for their overblown claims of effectiveness against the common cold: a malady whose cure remains elusive decades later. In 1956, *Consumer Reports* surveyed cold remedies and reported on their usefulness. Many (including laxatives, lemon drinks, and special diets) were of no medical value whatsoever. Others (such as nose drops, aspirin, and inhalers) offered only short-term relief. The best recommended course of action then was bed-rest, which prevented complications and kept the cold sufferer from infecting others.

In 1953, the American Medical Association (AMA) and the National Association of Radio and Television Broadcasters established a code which prohibited actors from playing doctors without being identified as actors, and restricted overuse of such words as "harmless," "safe," and "advertising material which describes or dramatizes distress." Nevertheless, drug manufacturers kept testing the limits of their advertising pitches.

Some of the dubious claims made by drug advertisers during the 1950s included:

> "Infra-Rub speeds up the flow of fresh, rich blood, thus helps drive away pain-causing pressure."

> "This doctor's discovery is called Sustamin 2-12. Doctors of three leading hospitals personally witnessed amazing results. They saw agonizing, crippling pain relieved day and night."

> "Javitol contains 85 percent choice coffee blends, combined with a vegetable extract that lets you literally drink that extra weight right off your body. Can you imagine?"

Greed and exploitation relating to health care were not confined to the advertising profession. In May 1957, a seven-year-old Long Island, New York, boy fell into a 21-foot-deep, 10-inch-wide well being dug for irrigation by his father. Fire fighters, police officers, and construction workers toiled feverishly to save him. After nineteen hours, the attending physician admitted that there was little hope for the boy's recovery. But the doctor was wrong. Five hours later, a construction worker lifted the boy out of the well. Once he was out of danger, the doctor presented his family with a $1,500 bill. People were furious. The boy's truck driver father earned $62 per week; his mother, a telephone operator, earned $42.

The doctor eventually withdrew the bill. Yet the incident served as an example of why Americans increasingly viewed those in the medical profession as impersonal and uncaring, and only concerned with collecting their rapidly rising fees.

❖ MENTAL ILLNESS: A LACK OF COMPASSION

On an average day in 1959, approximately eight hundred thousand Americans were in mental hospitals. Some never would leave. Indeed, such hospitals were little more than overcrowded warehouses where troubled individuals wasted away as they waited to die. Yet in mid-decade, there were only forty-seven hundred certified psychiatrists in the country, and only five hundred new ones were being trained each year.

In October and November 1956, *The Saturday Evening Post*, a popular national magazine, printed a six-part series on mental hospitals in America. The focus of the story was on one that appeared to be typical: Columbus State Hospital, formerly known as the Central Ohio Lunatic Asylum. Modern sensitivity may have demanded that the name be changed, but the sprawling facility was woefully understaffed. Of its 2,700 patients, just 385 were receiving therapy or treatment. Fourteen hundred were judged to be candidates for treatment if resources ever became available. The remaining nine hundred patients were labeled "custodial," meaning that they would be given minimal attention until they died.

Because it was inexpensive, the preferred form of treatment for many new patients was electroshock therapy, or EST. During EST, electric current is passed through the brain to induce convulsions that eventually have a calming effect on the patient. As the Columbus State Hospital's superintendent explained, "EST is our mainstay."

Wealthier mental patients were placed in private hospitals, where they received more individual psychotherapy. However, such hospital stays cost up to $1,600 per month, a hefty sum in the 1950s. At the time, only 2 percent of all mental hospital patients were in private institutions.

❖ POLIO: DESTROYING A DEADLY DISEASE

In the early 1950s, poliomyelitis (commonly known as polio) was a dreaded disease: a virus that caused a swelling of the gray matter of the spinal cord, resulting in the paralysis (inability to move or feel sensation) of different groups of muscles. President Franklin D. Roosevelt (1882–1945) had been stricken with the disease as an adult. However, its primary victims were children; thus, the disease also was known as "infantile paralysis." During the early years of the decade, polio reached epidemic proportions. In 1953, the National Foundation of Infantile Paralysis (NFIP), which provided funding for polio research, education, and patient assistance, announced that more polio cases had been reported during the past five years than in the previous twenty. In 1950, 28,386 severe cases were reported. By 1952, the number had risen to 55,000.

Polio is caused by the entry into the body of any one of three types of viruses. The virus goes into the body through the mouth and briefly resides in the bloodstream before taking one of two routes. If the patient is lucky, the virus makes its way into the bowels and subsequently is expelled from the body. In a less fortunate victim, the virus travels into the central nervous system where it damages cells in the brain stem or spinal cord. In these cases, the result is severe paralysis and sometimes death.

In the early 1950s, widespread rumors circulated regarding how polio originated and spread. The NFIP put the word out that fruit, insects, animals, and bad genes did not cause polio. Because polio tended to strike during the summer, the NFIP suggested that parents should send their

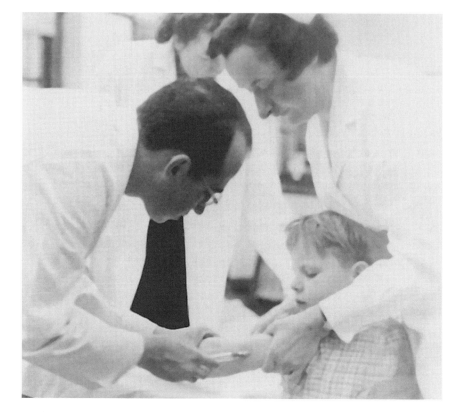

*Jonas Salk injecting a
child with the polio
vaccination. Before Salk
developed the vaccine,
polio caused many
deaths and cases of
paralysis in children.
Courtesy of the Library
of Congress.*

children only to summer camps that offered proper medical supervision.
Parents were advised not to allow children to mingle in crowds. While
swimming in public pools did not result in polio, crowds at pools might
increase the risk of transmission. As a result of this information, countless
public swimming pools were closed. Boys and girls often were confined to
their yards during the summer and in other seasons in regions where the
climate was warmer. Youngsters were encouraged to play quietly, because
sweating was thought to promote polio. They were discouraged from playing with anyone but their closest friends.

Jonas Salk (1914–1995) was propelled to international acclaim when
he developed the first successful polio vaccine in the early 1950s. In the
late 1940s, Salk became director of the University of Pittsburgh School of
Medicine's Virus Research Laboratory. During the course of a three-year
project sponsored by the NFIP, Salk demonstrated the existence of three
types of polioviruses. He determined that in order to be effective, a vaccine must work against all three. He then began working to develop such a
vaccine, using dead viruses suspended in mineral oil and formaldehyde.
Tests of the vaccine Salk created took place in 1953 and 1954. During

1954, 1.8 million schoolchildren were given the vaccine; they came to be known as "polio pioneers." Over 440,000 "pioneers" were given the real vaccine, which was injected into the bloodstream, while 210,000 were given placebos (dummy shots); the remaining children were observed as a control group. The tests were successful. Those who received the placebo contracted 3.5 times more cases of polio than those who had been given the vaccine. As a result, the mass immunization of American children began in 1955.

By the end of 1958, 200 million shots of what had become popularly known as the Salk vaccine had been given to Americans, starting with first graders. However, its benefits were limited. It immunized against polio for only about thirty months, at which point a second shot was required. Before the decade ended, Albert Sabin (1906–1993) developed a more effective vaccine: a "live-virus" one, made up of viruses that were too weak to cause the disease but strong enough to stimulate the human body to react against it for a longer time. Sabin first tested his vaccine on thirty prisoner volunteers in 1955. However, the thinking at the time was that the only good virus was a dead virus. So Sabin accepted the invitation of scientists from the Soviet Union to further test his vaccine in Russia. He successfully vaccinated millions of Soviet schoolchildren and, by the early 1960s, his vaccine had completely replaced the Salk vaccine. It provided nearly lifetime immunity from the disease. By the 1980s, fewer than ten cases of polio were reported in the United States each year.

Not surprisingly, children preferred the Sabin vaccine over the Salk version for one reason: It was taken orally, rather than by injection!

❖ RADIATION: A NEW WAY OF SEEING AND HEALING

One of the side benefits of nuclear research done during the 1950s in the name of national defense was that scientists came to understand the manner in which radiation works. Radiation is the process by which energy in the form of heat or light is emitted from molecules and atoms as they undergo internal transformation. Those researching the process and its effect discovered that controlled, low levels of radiation could be used for medical purposes.

Radiation was employed to assist in diagnosing cancer. Scientists observed that cancerous tumors absorbed radioactive material (substances that give off radiation) several times more readily than normal tissue. A patient who was suspected of having cancer was asked to swallow capsules filled with low-level radioactive material. After allowing time for digestion, a Geiger counter (an instrument that measures levels of radia-

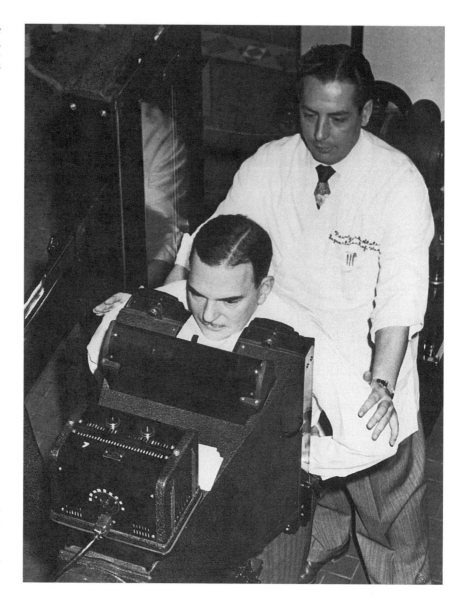

New York governor
Thomas E. Dewey
participating in a chest X-
ray demonstration.
Reproduced by permission of
the Corbis Corporation.

tion) was used on the outside of the abdomen. If the Geiger counter recorded unusually high levels of radioactivity, it was assumed that the reaction came from a cancerous tumor.

Radioactivity also was utilized in the healing process. In 1953, scientists unveiled a cobalt-ray machine on national television. This apparatus could send massive doses of radiation to a focused spot on a patient's lung, killing the targeted cancerous tissue. But because radiation treatments also destroy some healthy body cells, many people were concerned that treatments might be as deadly as they were beneficial.

❖ SHAPING UP AMERICA'S YOUTH

According to the results of a 1957 study testing the "minimum muscular fitness" of American children, over half of the nation's young people were not physically fit. When the same test was administered to a group of European students, more than 90 percent passed.

President Dwight Eisenhower (1890–1969), a former U.S. Army general, considered the nation's physical fitness a key to national security. To address what he labeled the "fitness gap," he created the President's Council on Youth Fitness. The council advised schools and communities to provide additional opportunities for organized sports and outdoor physical activity.

The irony was that the decline in American fitness was a direct result of the country's progress. Because of labor-saving devices found in many American homes, children had fewer and less-strenuous chores; for example, dishwashers and washing machines and dryers now automatically cleaned and dried dishes and clothes. Increased automobile traffic often made walking or bicycling to school too dangerous, and children were likely to ride school buses in many fast-growing communities. The growth of cities and suburbs led to a decline in space for children to play. Finally, children increasingly preferred to remain inside and watch television rather than go outside and hit baseballs or jump rope.

❖ TRANQUILIZERS: SIMPLE SOLUTIONS FOR COMPLEX PROBLEMS?

During the 1950s, America became a nation of pill-poppers. As scientists discovered new drugs to combat illness, Americans came to believe that pill-taking was a simple and effective means of feeling better. Among the era's most popular pills were tranquilizers, whose ingredients slowed down the action of the central nervous system and thus reduced nervous tension and anxiety. In 1956 alone, doctors wrote thirty-five million prescriptions for tranquilizers; a rate of one every second. Anxious patients struggling to cope with the stresses of modern life paid $150 million to get their pills.

One of the decade's most popular tranquilizers was called Miltown. It was developed by the drug company Ludwig and Piech; a competing company, Wyeth Laboratories, marketed the tranquilizer under the name Equinal. The pill was touted as a nonhabit-forming cure for anxiety and nervous tension. It achieved its effect approximately forty-five minutes after intake. The result was a satisfying sensation caused by muscle relaxation.

When Miltown and Equinal first were marketed in 1955, they were instant successes. Both were prescribed for illnesses ranging from alcoholism to insomnia, in addition to simple nervous tension. However, some in the medical profession were concerned that these tranquilizers were being prescribed too casually and haphazardly. In 1957, *Time* magazine reported that a woman in Beverly Hills, California, asked her doctor to prescribe tranquilizers for her daughter "who needed them to get through the trying first week of her honeymoon." A woman in Boston asked her pharmacist for a bottle of "happiness pills." The following year, the president of the American Medical Association (AMA) warned that "modern man cannot solve his problems of daily living with a pill."

❖ TUBERCULOSIS: THE DEMISE OF A DISEASE

In the 1950s, tuberculosis (TB) had long been a frightening and deadly disease. TB is a bacterial disease that affects the lungs and often results from unsanitary living conditions. Because tuberculosis is highly contagious, victims were isolated in special hospitals called sanatoriums. The death rate from the disease in 1950 was only 11 percent of what it had been a half-century earlier. Still, 33,633 people died of tuberculosis that year. The discovery of antibiotics to combat the disease helped to further reduce its death rate. Furthermore, a blood test was developed early in the decade that accurately detected the disease in its early stages.

By mid-decade, the number of deaths from tuberculosis had been cut in half, and as the years passed, they kept steadily decreasing. All of this signified the beginning of the end of TB as a formidable public health problem.

For More Information

BOOKS

Berger, Melvin. *The Artificial Heart*. New York: Franklin Watts, 1987.

Bredeson, Carmen. *Jonas Salk: Discoverer of the Polio Vaccine*. Hillside, NJ: Enslow Publishers, 1993.

Clayton, Lawrence, Ph.D. *Tranquilizers*. Springfield, NJ: Enslow Publishers, 1997.

Day, Nancy. *Killer Superbugs: The Story of Drug-Resistant Diseases*. Berkeley Heights, NJ: Enslow Publishers, 2001.

De Angelis, Gina. *Nicotine and Cigarettes*. Philadelphia: Chelsea House, 1999.

Hyde, Margaret O. *Know About Tuberculosis*. New York: Walker & Company, 1994.

Kehret, Peg. *Small Steps: The Year I Got Polio*. Morton Grove, IL: Albert Whitman & Company, 1996.

Landau, Elaine. *Tuberculosis.* New York: Franklin Watts, 1995.

McPherson, Stephanie Sammartino. *Jonas Salk: Conquering Polio.* Minneapolis, MN: Lerner Publications, 2002.

Morgan, Sally. *Smoking.* Austin, TX: Raintree Steck-Vaughn, 2002.

Murphy, Jack and Wendy Murphy. *Nuclear Medicine.* New York: Chelsea House, 1994.

Nardo, Don. *Germs: Mysterious Microorganisms.* San Diego: Lucent Books, 1991.

Pringle, Laurence. *Smoking: A Risky Business.* New York: Morrow Junior Books, 1996.

Roleff, Tamara L., and Mary E. Williams, eds. *Tobacco and Smoking: Opposing Viewpoints.* San Diego: Greenhaven Press, 1998.

Silverstein, Alvin, Virginia Silverstein, and Robert Silverstein. *Tuberculosis.* Hillside, NJ: Enslow Publishers, 1994.

Tocci, Salvatore. *Alexander Fleming: The Man Who Discovered Penicillin.* Berkeley Heights, NJ: Enslow Publishers, 2002.

Yancey, Diane. *Tuberculosis.* Brookfield, CT: Twenty-First Century Books, 2001.

WEB SITES

American Experience/A Brilliant Madness. http://www.pbs.org/wgbh/amex/nash/timeline/timeline2.html (accessed on August 9, 2002).

Fear of Polio in the 1950s. http://www.inform.umd.edu/HONR/HONR269J/.WWW/projects/sokol.html (accessed on August 9, 2002).

The 1950s: Era of the Mass Disease Campaign. http://www.unicef.org/sowc96/1950s.htm (accessed on August 9, 2002).

1950s Timeline. http://www.cdc.gov/eis/about/timeline.htm (accessed on August 9, 2002).

Science and Technology

1950: The Sulzer weaving machine, employing an automatic loom, begins modern commercial production of cloth.

1950: Scientists at the University of Wisconsin implant an embryo (early form of life developed from a fertilized egg) in the uterus of a cow.

1951: A Swedish dentist constructs the first air-powered, high-speed dental drill.

1951: Chrysler introduces the first production-model car with power steering.

1951: The nuclear testing station at Arco, Idaho, produces electricity from nuclear power.

1951: Marion Donovan develops "The Boater," the first disposable diaper.

1951: **April** Remington-Rand sells the first commercially available computer, the UNIVAC I.

1952: George Jorgensen, a U.S. Army private, travels to Denmark where he undergoes an operation to change his sex and emerges as Christine Jorgensen.

1952: **November 1** The first full-scale test of a crude hydrogen bomb takes place on Elugelab Island in the Pacific Ocean.

1953: The Raytheon Company patents a "high-frequency dielectric heating apparatus," otherwise known as a microwave oven.

1953: Mathematician Norbert Wiener introduces the new field of "cybernetics" (the study of control and communication in the animal and the machine).

1954: Charles H. Townes proves that light energy can be amplified. The phenomenon is called a laser.

1954: The first regularly operated bevatron (atom smasher) is built in Berkeley, California.

1954: The commercial transistor radio debuts on the U.S. market.

1954: Odeco, Inc. employs the first mobile, submersible oil-drilling unit for offshore drilling in the Gulf of Mexico.

1954: Bell Laboratories develops the photovoltaic cell, which converts sunlight into electricity.

1955: Scientists first hear radio emissions originating on the planet Jupiter.

1955: Multiple-track recording, in which songs are recorded with voice on one track and music on another, is introduced, resulting in the commercialization of stereophonic sound equipment and phonograph records.

1955: The Field-Ion microscope, which can indirectly see individual atoms, is developed.

1955: A home freezer that can maintain a minus-27-degree Fahrenheit temperature is introduced.

1955: **January** The nuclear submarine *Nautilus* makes its first dive, lasting one hour, in Long Island Sound.

1955: **June** The British ship *Monarch* begins laying transatlantic cable between Great Britain and the United States.

1955: **October–November** Pan American Airways purchases Boeing 707 and Douglas DC-8 jet aircraft, signaling the birth of the commercial jet age in the United States.

1956: Fifteen thousand women in Puerto Rico and Haiti volunteer to test the effectiveness and safety of the oral contraceptive birth control pill.

1956: Bell Laboratories produces a transistorized computer.

1956: Burroughs markets the E-101 desktop computer for scientists and mathematicians.

1956: The "Ampex" system produces taped television shows of comparable quality to live shows.

1956: The Mid-Oceanic Ridge, a formation of mountains and rifts that circles the world under the oceans, is discovered.

1956: **September 25** The first eastbound telephone call is completed using the transatlantic cable.

1957: Doppler navigation, a device for accurately determining aircraft position and airspeed, makes civil aviation safer.

1957: Hoover develops a spin clothes dryer.

1957: Fifty-six countries participate in the International Geophysical Year, sponsored by the International Council of Scientific Unions.

1957: **October 4** The Soviet Union launches its *Sputnik* satellite.

1958: The first U.S. artificial satellite orbits Earth.

1958: Bifocal contact lenses are developed.

1958: Pan American Airway flies the first commercial transatlantic route in a jet.

1958: **July** The *Explorer IV* satellite verifies the presence of a radiation belt around Earth.

1959: The first commercial copy machine is introduced by Xerox.

1959: Transistors are placed on silicon chips for the first time.

1959: Sony produces the first transistorized black-and-white television set in the United States.

1959: **April 25** The Saint Lawrence Seaway, an engineering marvel that provides sea access from the Atlantic Ocean to the Great Lakes, opens to shipping.

Overview

During the 1950s, dramatic advances in an array of technologies reshaped American culture and transformed the manner in which Americans viewed civilization. More and more families owned television sets, on which they increasingly depended for news and entertainment. While most TV sets picked up only black-and-white signals, the first color TVs were produced and the first broadcasts presented "in living color" were aired. Improvements in magnetic tape quality resulted in an increase in the taping of television programs (before tape, all shows were aired live). A transatlantic cable was laid between Europe and North America, allowing for improvements in telephone communication between the continents. Jet-propelled aircraft were introduced, leading to nonstop air travel across and between continents. Scientific advances were made in a range of disciplines, from geology to genetics. New products were developed, from photocopy machines to oral contraceptive birth control pills, long-playing records (LPs) to Liquid Paper. The earliest video game was even invented in 1958!

One of the decade's watershed events was the marketing of the first commercially produced computer, the UNIVAC I. By contemporary standards, the UNIVAC was huge and physically imposing. It was purchased by large corporations and government agencies; the concept of the personal home computer would not be realized for decades. While many at the time were fascinated by computers, others feared these new machines. Would the advent of computer technology lead to a future in which machines ruled humankind? Another momentous development was the evolution and commercial marketing of the transistor. First developed in 1947, the transistor (a small, durable electronic device used for sound amplification and switching) became a key component in a host of products, including television sets, computers, radios, and hearing aids.

On a more ominous note, the development of the H-Bomb (hydrogen bomb) accelerated during the early 1950s, as the cold war escalated between the United States and Soviet Russia. The H-Bomb was more powerful and deadly than the A-Bomb (atomic bomb) that had exploded over Hiroshima and Nagasaki in 1945, ending World War II. Some in the scientific community, like physicist Edward Teller, favored the employment of nuclear technology in weaponry. Others, such as J. Robert Oppenheimer, the physicist who headed the Manhattan Project, which developed the atomic bomb, stressed that the technology should be used only for peaceful purposes. Meanwhile, the development of Intercontinental Ballistic Missiles (ICBMs) allowed for the launching of nuclear warheads that could speed across Earth and destroy their targets. Such technological advances immeasurably aided the escalation of the nuclear arms race. Then on October 4, 1957, the space age was born when the Soviets launched *Sputnik,* the first satellite to orbit Earth.

Scientific and technological progress was making everyday life more pleasant and comfortable, particularly for those whose financial resources allowed them to fly across the world in jet aircraft or place telephone calls across continents. At the same time, many feared that much of this new technology also might be employed to wage war, and perhaps destroy civilization.

Chester Carlson (1906–1968)   During his career as a patent attorney, Chester Carlson had to tediously hand-copy material. This experience allowed him to envision the need for a copying machine, so he set out to invent one. Carlson's creation, developed after years of experimentation, was named "xerography" (*xeros* is Greek for "dry"; *graphos* is Greek for "writing"). It was unsuccessfully marketed in 1949 and 1950. A more sophisticated version was developed in 1959. This machine became a spectacular success. In 1961, the company that produced it changed its name to Xerox Corporation.   *Photo reproduced by permission of the Corbis Corporation.*

Grace Murray Hopper (1906–1992)   Grace Murray Hopper's ground-breaking efforts to devise computer programs and language changed the computer forever. During World War II (1939–45), she learned to program the Mark I, the world's first large digital computer. After the war, she worked at Remington-Rand, the company that marketed the UNIVAC computer. In the 1950s, she created a computer program that translated instructions written in more complex language. Her program provided the bridge between simple commands and the intricate set of purely electronic, machine-language commands that speak directly to parts of the computer. She also developed a programming language called COBOL, which made business applications on computers practical.   *Photo reproduced courtesy of the Library of Congress.*

Alfred Kinsey (1897–1956)   In 1938, Alfred Kinsey became chairman of a Indiana University committee whose mission was to create the content of a new course on marriage. This led him to conduct what would become a landmark study on sexuality: an aspect of human biology that never before had been given scientific scrutiny. Kinsey began collecting data and completing the first of 7,985 interviews in which he charted individual sexual histories. He eventually published two ground-breaking books, *Sexual Behavior in the Human Male* (1948) and *Sexual Behavior in the Human Female* (1953).   *Photo reproduced courtesy of the Library of Congress.*

Arthur Kornberg (1918–) Arthur Kornberg's illustrious career in scientific research began when he studied the chemical bilirubin, and how an excessive amount of it in the bloodstream results in jaundice (a yellowing of the white parts of the eyes). Then he explored the role of intestinal bacteria in providing vitamins in the diet. Next he moved on to work with enzymes (large proteins that speed up chemical reactions), focusing on those associated with DNA synthesis (production). The sum total of his research aided immeasurably in the evolution of the field of molecular biology.

Margaret Sanger (1879–1966) During the 1950s, Margaret Sanger was partially responsible for the development of the oral contraceptive pill. However, this accomplishment was a minute part of her life's work. She believed that women had to have control of reproduction as a matter of health and well-being, and she crusaded for their right to receive contraception information. In doing so, she battled a range of opposing forces, from the Roman Catholic Church to such organizations as the New York Society for the Suppression of Vice. It was Sanger who coined the term *birth control* and formed the organization that eventually became the International Planned Parenthood Federation. In 1952, she became its first director.

Wernher von Braun (1912–1977) Wernher von Braun always was fascinated by astronomy and rocketry. By the time he earned his engineering degree in Germany in 1932, he had staged eighty-five rocket test launches. Before coming to the United States in 1945, he designed the first self-contained missile, which Germany employed against Great Britain during World War II (1939–45). Von Braun headed the research team that launched the first U.S. satellite in 1958. Eventually, he helped develop the Saturn rocket employed in the Apollo moon landing. For much of his adult life, von Braun was the world's foremost rocket scientist. *Photo reproduced courtesy of the Library of Congress.*

Topics in the News

❖ FROM COLOR TV TO MAGNETIC TAPE, TRANSISTORS TO TRANSATLANTIC CABLES

During the 1950s, technological innovations resulted in the rapid improvement of mass communication. By the end of the decade, television had replaced radio, newspapers, and magazines as the primary source of entertainment and information for most Americans. Advancements in electronics made television sets affordable and thus available to almost everyone in the United States. For years, electronics engineers had been developing systems for sending and receiving broadcast signals in color. On January 1, 1954, the Tournament of Roses Parade, originating in Pasadena, California, became the first national coast-to-coast "colorcast," or television programming broadcast in color. The American Telephone and Telegraph Company (AT&T) established a color network of twenty-two cities, to which the Radio Corporation of America (RCA) sent the equipment needed to receive the color signal. The parade was presented by the National Broadcasting Company (NBC). Despite the momentous nature of the event in broadcasting history, only several thousand viewers across the country had the equipment to see this groundbreaking telecast.

Occasionally during the early 1950s, television series were shot on film and edited before being broadcast. *I Love Lucy* (1951–57), a classic situation comedy, is the most famous of the era's filmed television shows. At the time, many TV programs were presented live. Any and all mistakes occurring during the broadcast, from technical glitches to actors forgetting or misreading their lines, were seen by audiences. During this original transmission, a television monitor on which the program appeared was used to film the program. Called kinescopes, these films were used to rebroadcast the program in different time zones. Kinescopes usually were visually fuzzy and second-rate in quality. However, the evolution of high-quality magnetic tape (a ribbon of thin plastic employed in the use of magnetic recording, the process by which sounds and images were inscribed onto the tape) allowed for the taping of television shows. If an actor forgot a line, the scene simply could be retaped. The footage was edited during the postproduction process and could be rebroadcast at the convenience of the television network.

In 1947, Walter Brattain (1902–1987), John Bardeen (1908–1991), and William Shockley (1910–1989) of the Bell Laboratories created the first transistor. Their discovery was one of the most significant developments in twentieth-century technology, and it resulted in the birth of a multibillion-dollar industry. Transistors soon were employed in a variety of products, from computers and television sets to hearing aids. The device allowed for the development and mass-marketing of small, portable radios (commonly known as transistor radios). In 1959, almost half of the ten million radios produced in the United States were powered by transistors. Seven years earlier, Western Electric engineers had even produced a transistor wristwatch. It was presented as a gift to Chester Gould (1900–1985), creator of the *Dick Tracy* comic strip. (In 1946, Gould had equipped his fictional crime-busting hero with a special two-way, voice-activated video phone worn around the wrist.)

Telephone communication improved greatly during the decade. American Telephone and Telegraph (AT&T), the British Post Office (which ran the British telephone system), and the Canadian Overseas Telecommunications Corporation sponsored operation of the first transatlantic cable line to be used for telephone communication. It consisted of two specially coated and insulated 2,500-mile-long wire bundles laid along the floor of the Atlantic Ocean. One was used for eastbound communication, the other for westbound. The cable was designed to carry thirty-six telephone conversations at a time, and up to 1,200 calls per day. It was built at a cost of $40 million. By 1956, it was possible for Americans and Europeans to telephone one another using this system. However, phone calls were expensive. Cable calls cost $12 during the day and $9 at night for three minutes of connection time.

Finally, in 1950, the Aircall Corporation of New York marketed a radio pager (beeper). The first person to be paged was none other than a physician on a golf course!

❖ THE COMPUTER COMES OF AGE

The first commercial computers went on sale in the United States in the early 1950s. Originally, they were designed as powerful calculators. Not surprisingly, in 1951, the U.S. Census Bureau became the very first purchaser of the UNIVAC I, the initial digital computer available on the commercial marketplace. The UNIVAC (Universal Automatic Computer) was nothing like the personal computer (PC) of today. It measured fourteen feet by seven feet by nine feet, the size of a small bedroom. A set of five thousand vacuum tubes made it operable. Its internal memory was one thousand words. Software (stored programs) existed only in a primitive form. At the time, social observers predicted that by the year 2000 perhaps fifty of these huge, expensive machines would be in use! It was thought that only the governments of affluent nations, major corporations, and well-funded scientific organizations would be able to afford computers.

Major changes were made in the computer between 1950 and 1959. The development and availability of the transistor led to the replacement of vacuum tubes in the computer's processing unit. Transistors also made the computer easier to miniaturize, allowing its imposing size to be reduced without any loss of function. Another important change involved the development of software. The introduction of magnetic-core memory increased the internal information-storage capacity of a computer about eightfold. This innovation allowed computers to remember more complicated routines of calculation.

The advent of the computer age inspired anxiety in many who viewed computers as bewildering and frightening machines that had the potential

The UNIVAC computer was the first American commercial computer. Reproduced by permission of the Corbis Corporation.

to run amok and take power over their creators. Additionally, it was feared that the employment of computers might have a devastating impact on the economy. If a handful of computer-literate individuals and their machines could replace thousands of clerks, typists, and bookkeepers, where would these newly jobless workers find employment?

These fears were contemplated and scrutinized in popular culture. *The Desk Set*, a comedy which opened on Broadway in 1955 and became a motion picture two years later, was the story of an efficiency expert who installs a computer in a broadcasting company's research department. The department's workers cringe at the thought of being replaced by a machine and assume that they soon will be unemployed. A primary "character" in *2001: A Space Odyssey* (1968), one of the most celebrated films of the late 1960s, is a computer named Hal that manipulates and outwits astronauts on board a spaceship. In countless films and television show episodes, computers were portrayed as monstrous machines that comically malfunctioned, resulting in their uncontrollably spewing out thousands of computer cards. Many people who acknowledged the benefits of computerizing some functions were still intimidated by computer technology. They feared they would never learn the language to communicate in a computerized world. Television shows satirizing computers often featured flustered characters who failed in their attempt to operate the machine and haplessly scampered about as punch cards spewed across the office.

On the night of the 1952 presidential election, Americans were allowed to glimpse the manner in which computers eventually would affect their lives. Until this election, voting returns were counted by hand, precinct by precinct. This was a long, tedious process that sometimes lasted for days. Furthermore, election predictions were unsystematic and untrustworthy. With the growing popularity of television, an expectation arose that the election's winner could be determined and announced to viewers within a reasonable amount of time. For this purpose, the Columbia Broadcasting System (CBS) approached Remington-Rand about employing their adding machines during its election coverage. In return, CBS would advertise the company's products. A company employee suggested that CBS instead utilize a different Remington-Rand product: its new UNIVAC computer. Since computers themselves were so new, no one ever had tried to enter the massive amounts of data involved in predicting a national election. Additionally, newscasters doubted the computer's accuracy. Observed CBS newscaster Walter Cronkite (1916–), "Actually, we're not depending too much on this machine. It may turn out to be just a sideshow…"

Just to be safe, three computers were employed on the night of the election. The primary machine was shown on television. A second checked the results from the first. The third was ready for use on a standby basis. At 9:00 P.M., after tallying and analyzing three million votes, or 7 percent of the total votes, UNIVAC predicted that Dwight Eisenhower (1890–1969), the Republican Party candidate, would win in a landslide over Adlai Stevenson (1900–1965), his Democratic opponent. It predicted that Eisenhower would win forty-three states, for a total of 438 electoral votes. Having such a prediction so early in the election was deemed impossible. CBS decided to withhold announcing the information, to avoid embarrassment in case it was incorrect. Meanwhile, analysts and programmers busily set out to determine what had gone wrong with UNIVAC. The computer's mathematical formulas were revised and revised again and, at 10:00 P.M., UNIVAC declared that each candidate would win twenty-four states (in 1952, the country consisted of forty-eight states; Alaska and Hawaii had not yet achieved statehood), with Eisenhower earning 270 electoral votes to 261 for Stevenson. CBS broadcast these figures. By 11:00 P.M. it became obvious that the computer's original figures were closer to the truth. The network finally admitted that UNIVAC had made the earlier prediction, but it had not been considered credible. The final count: Eisenhower won 442 electoral votes. UNIVAC's accurate prediction so soon after the polls closed fascinated many Americans, and only hinted at the power and potential of the computer.

❖ COMPUTER LANGUAGE: A NEW WAY OF COMMUNICATING

The advent of computers during the 1950s brought about the need for a way to "communicate" with computers to tell them what to do and how to do it. The solution was computer language. Advances in computer languages made it possible to program computers so that their functions became varied enough to appeal to a broad range of users. These changes began to occur during the decade.

Computer languages were based on a system of logic and mathematics called Boolean algebra. Using a simple numbering system, Boolean algebra allows computer programmers to talk to their machines in terms the machine understands. All communication is expressed by employing a set of switches operated by electric current.

Formula Translation Language (FORTRAN), introduced in 1956, was a computer language that allowed scientists to program computers. Common Business-Oriented Language (COBOL) was developed for computers used in business. A language called LISt Processing (LISP) was employed by scientists at the Massachusetts Institute of Technology (MIT) in the late 1950s to develop computers that would respond intelligently to commands.

A Secretary's Job in a 1950s' Office

Before the introduction of word processors and copying machines, offices were far more labor-intensive places. The simple chore of typing a letter was demanding because errors were difficult to correct. One innovation that addressed this problem was a product called Liquid Paper (sometimes referred to as "white out"), which allowed secretaries to paint over errors before retyping. Another was correction paper. When a mistake was made, the typist backed up, inserted correction paper, and retyped the misspelling so that it would be "whited out" and therefore difficult to see. Then the secretary typed again, correcting the error.

Two types of copying machines also were introduced: the thermofax, which copied on coated paper; and xerography, which copied on plain paper. With regard to duplicating documents, a necessity in most any office, these machines greatly simplified a secretary's job.

❖ EXPLORING THE NATURE OF HEREDITY

Scientifically, sex has a single purpose: to pass on one's genes to future generations. The genes are the basis of heredity. Deoxyribonucleic acid (DNA) is located in the nucleus of cells. In turn, the DNA is packaged into structures called chromosomes. Every species of animal and plant has a certain number of such chromosomes within each of its cells.

In the early 1950s, very little was known about genes and how they function. Within the realm of genetics, the decade's major achievement was determining the structure of DNA, which allowed scientists to conclude that DNA contained the code for genes. Rosalind Franklin (1920–1958), working at King's College in London with Maurice H. F. Wilkins (1916–), studied DNA by bombarding molecules with X rays and reflecting the resulting images onto a photographic screen. American biochemist James D. Watson (1928–) and English biophysicist Francis H.C. Crick (1916–) took these findings and determined that DNA is composed of four bases (adenine, thymine, guanine, and cytosine) attached to a sugar-phosphate backbone. Furthermore, they determined the manner in which these bases interact. These discoveries gave birth to the field of molecular biology, in which researchers try to determine exactly which genes cause certain characteristics in living organisms.

In 1956, researchers Joe Hin Tjio (1919–2001) and Albert Levan (1905–) concluded a study in which they took photographs of many cells in the human embryo. Their efforts proved that such cells have forty-six chromosomes each, and germ cells have twenty-three chromosomes. Three years later, another researcher, Jerome Lejeune (1926–1994), completed a study of individuals affected with what then was known as mongolism (and today is called Down's Syndrome, a condition which develops during pregnancy and is characterized by mental deficiency and some recognizable physical characteristics). Lejeune found that children suffering from Down's Syndrome had forty-seven chromosomes instead of forty-six.

❖ FOSSIL DATING: EXPLORING GEOLOGIC AGES

During the 1950s, scientists made important advances in their ability to accurately date ancient rocks and fossils (remains of plants or animals that have been preserved in Earth's crust). Long after an organism's demise, the quantity of radioactive elements remaining in its dead carbo-based tissue can be measured and compared to nonradioactive material to determine how long it has been since the organism's death. However, standard radioactive dating processes such as carbon dating, discovered in 1948, would not work on most fossils. The reason: fossilized remains contain very little carbon, if any.

The only methods of dating fossils in the early 1950s were crude. A scientist might date a new specimen based on a general knowledge of the time period in which it originated. Or the scientist might know the location of the fossil when it was recovered, and guess its age based on an estimation of how long it took layers of earth to form over it. Such estimates were not very accurate.

To determine the age of rocks and fossils, a group of geologists and physicists at the University of California-Berkeley devised a new radioactive-potassium dating system, which proved much more reliable than previous measures. As it decays, radioactive potassium forms a gas known as argon. Because the potassium is also found in small amounts in rock, it was theoretically possible to measure the amounts that had been converted to argon. This measurement was difficult, but by using painstaking extraction methods and a highly sensitive monitoring device called a mass spectrometer, the Berkeley group succeeded in developing an acceptable method.

❖ THE H-BOMB: EXPANDING THE ATOMIC AGE

The H-Bomb (or hydrogen bomb) was the product of scientific research that evolved after the development of the A-Bomb (atomic bomb), which had been dropped on Hiroshima and Nagasaki in Japan near the end of World War II (1939–45). Atomic bomb technology is based on nuclear *fission* (the *splitting* of the atom, resulting in the release of massive amounts of energy). However, H-Bomb technology is based on nuclear *fusion* (the *joining* of atoms, which also releases massive amounts of energy). The H-Bomb can release even more energy than the A-Bomb, but it requires considerably more force and power to detonate.

The awesome, destructive capacity of the A-Bomb shocked the world, and there was a heated debate concerning the morality of its use. The thought of an even more powerful weapon was repugnant to many people, who were frightened by the potential that some day a bomb capable of destroying all civilization might be developed. Nuclear scientists were divided into two camps: those who opposed the development of nuclear power for weaponry, led by J. Robert Oppenheimer (1904–1967); and those who favored perfecting the H-Bomb, led by Edward Teller (1908–). This debate was fueled by the beginning of the Cold War between the United States and the Soviet Union (U.S.S.R.). In 1948, the Soviets successfully tested an A-Bomb. The following year, reports of their substantial progress in developing an H-Bomb reached the United States. These events caused President Harry S Truman (1884–1972) to side with Teller. Oppenheimer, meanwhile, had been the head of the Manhattan Project, which had developed the atomic bomb during World War II. He had come to believe that nuclear power only should be employed for peaceful purposes. However, his friendships with liberals during the Red Scare that swept across America during the early 1950s resulted in his being labeled a security risk. Oppenheimer was not allowed to continue his scientific inquiry in this direction.

Electronics: A New Kind of Plaything

During World War II (1939–45), physicist Willy Higginbotham helped develop a radar system for the B-29 bomber and contributed to research on the atomic bomb. After the war, he worked at the Brookhaven National Laboratory, a center for nuclear research on Long Island, New York, operated by the U.S Atomic Energy Commission. As director of the instrumentation division, Higginbotham decided to concoct something interesting for visitors to view as they toured the laboratory. In 1958, he took spare parts from equipment around his office, hooked them together, and created a game. On a five-inch screen, he electronically drew a tennis court. A bouncing dot of light represented the ball. On each side of the gadget were two controls, a button and knob. When the button was pushed, the ball moved across the court; the knob controlled the ball's speed. Higginbotham saw no commercial application for his concoction. Even if he had, he could not have patented it because he was a U.S. government employee and he had created his game on government time. Unknowingly, Higginbotham's creation would, decades later, revolutionize the entertainment industry. He had invented the world's first video game!

H-Bomb development progressed, and in November 1952 a crude version was exploded on Elugelab Island in the Pacific. The Soviets followed with a more sophisticated device, which they tested in August 1953. In March 1954, the United States tested the first H-Bomb capable of being dropped from an airplane onto an enemy. The result was that both superpowers could threaten to shower each other with awesomely destructive bombs. The scientists had done their work. It now was up to the diplomats and politicians to argue over how the power to destroy the world would be used.

❖ ICBM: LONG-RANGE BOMBING CAPABILITY

"ICBM" stands for Intercontinental Ballistic Missile, a long-range missile whose operation depends upon the scientific laws of flight trajectory (the curved path that a body, such as a rocket, takes as it soars through space). The ICBM concept was born during the 1950s, when the United States worked to develop new and more powerful bombs to maintain its military superiority over the Soviet Union. As the arms race progressed, it became clear that a new, highly effective delivery system for warheads had to be developed.

From the late 1940s on, both the United States and the Soviet Union engaged in a frantic race to be the first to develop rockets capable of delivering atomic weaponry from domestic launchpads to strategic enemy sites. Both sides were quick to develop short-range rockets, which were useful on battlefields but not for exploding an atomic or hydrogen bomb on an enemy half a globe away. The Soviets produced the first ICBM, with a 6,000-mile range. This "Sapwood" rocket was operational in 1957. The Americans were already testing the "Thor" and "Atlas" ICBMs, and were developing the "Minuteman" rocket.

❖ JET AIRCRAFT: FLYING AT THE SPEED OF SOUND

In the 1950s, more Americans than ever before traveled by air for business and pleasure. Also during the decade, jet aircraft replaced slower, propeller-driven planes. In the military, the change was swift; in civilian aviation, it took place more slowly.

During World War II (1939–45), the United States government accelerated research and development of high-performance jet aircraft in order to counter the German air force's jet fighters. While American pilots never flew jets during the war, the U.S. Air Force tested a number of jet and rocket-powered planes from 1942 onward. The jet age began in America on October 14, 1947, when a Bell X-1 rocket plane, piloted by Charles E. "Chuck" Yeager (1923–), reached a speed of 964 miles per hour at an altitude of 42,000 feet. The Bell X-1 demonstrated that aircraft could fly faster than the speed of sound (760 miles per hour at sea level) without disintegrating. Still, jet aircraft lacked the range and engine life of propeller aircraft.

During the Korean War (1950–53), the U.S. Air Force and U.S. Navy employed large numbers of jet (as well as propeller) aircraft. Most American fighter planes were jets, but none of them (including the Lockheed P-80 "Shooting Star," the North American F-86A "Sabre," and the Grumman F9F-2 "Panther") could fly at the speed of sound in level flight. American bombers were powered by either piston engine or turboprop (a jet turbine driving a high-speed propeller). The lone American multi-engine jet bomber employed in the war was the B-45 "Tornado." The large strategic jet bombers, the Boeing B-47 and B-52, became operational in 1951 and 1952, but they did not see combat in Korea.

Initially, U.S. commercial airlines did not have much faith in the reliability of jet-powered aircraft. For one thing, the DH.106 "Comet I," the first commercial jet aircraft (operated by Great Britain's de Havilland aircraft company), was earning negative publicity. Early models suffered from structural problems that resulted in fractures in the fuselage. Then on January 10 and April 8, 1954, two "Comet I" jets crashed in the Mediterranean Sea, forcing de Havilland to temporarily ground its fleet until diagnostic technicians could uncover the plane's structural flaws.

In spite of these problems, officials at the Boeing and Douglas aircraft companies remained convinced that the future of commercial flying would include jet aircraft. Boeing developed what eventually would become the first American passenger jet, the Model 707. The earliest competitor to the 707, the Douglas DC-8, also competed for commercial contracts. Pan American Airways gave the industry a vote of confidence in 1955 when it purchased a number of Boeing 707s and DC-8s, the latter of which it planned to use for its new, nonstop transatlantic flights.

The jet age in commercial aviation had arrived. By decade's end, transcontinental jet passenger aircraft (along with supersonic fighters in the military) were the norm in aviation.

❖ LPs AND "45s": MORE FOR YOUR LISTENING PLEASURE

During the 1950s, emerging technology revolutionized the record industry. Until June 1948, home listening to recorded music required a forgiving ear and a vivid imagination. At the time, records were all ten or twelve inches in diameter; they were nicknamed "78s," because they played on Victrolas (record players) at 78 revolutions per minute (rpm). These records broke easily. They scratched at the slightest touch, which made them skip during playback. They quickly wore out after repeated play. By today's standards, their sound quality was terrible.

In 1948, Columbia Records introduced unbreakable, scratch-resistant (but far from scratch-proof) vinylite records in ten and twelve-inch versions that played at 33 1/3 rpm. At the most, about four minutes of material could fit onto each side of a "78." Columbia's records could hold twenty-five minutes worth of music on each side. For this reason, they were called long-playing records, or LPs. Meanwhile, RCA-Victor marketed 6 $\frac{7}{8}$-inch discs called "45s," because they played at 45 rpm. Generally one song, running from between two and three minutes, was recorded on each side of a "45." Still, they were an improvement over 78s because they were more durable and offered superior sound quality. A "45" was further distinguished from a "78" and LP by the hole in its center, which was one-and-one-half-inches in diameter; "78s" and LPs had only quarter-inch spindle holes. During the 1950s, LPs (albums) and "45s" (singles) became the record industry standard.

❖ *SPUTNIK* AND THE SPACE RACE

On October 4, 1957, Americans were shocked to learn that the Soviet Union, their nation's foe in the ongoing cold war, had successfully launched the *Sputnik* satellite. The event predated a similar planned U.S. launch by several months. The *Sputnik* was a small metal ball that did not do much of anything. It weighed 185 pounds, measured twenty-three inches in diameter, and orbited Earth every ninety minutes. It carried two tiny radio transmitters that produced a repetitive beeping noise as it traveled. Yet *Sputnik* demonstrated that the Soviets were capable of producing rockets that also could send nuclear weapons through space. As the satellite circled Earth, Americans looked skyward in wonder and fear. Many were convinced that *Sputnik* presaged a Soviet atomic attack.

The United States quickly responded to the Soviet launch. In 1958, the government created the National Aeronautics and Space Administration (NASA). In 1958 and 1959, America launched nineteen satellites. Both nations attempted to launch a satellite into lunar orbit, in order to

Two monkeys, Baker and Able, were sent into space aboard the Jupiter missile. *Photograph by Vince Finnigan. Reproduced by permission of Vince Finnigan and Getty Images.*

study the moon's surface. Both the Soviet *Metcha* (or *Lunik*) and the American *Pioneer IV* missed the moon and went into solar orbit, where the Sun's heat eventually turned them into cinders. In 1959, the Soviets achieved a lunar orbit with its *Lunik III*.

Animals also played important roles as passengers on these early satellites. They were employed to test the effects of outer space on living organisms. These animal visitors to outer space were named and celebrated. In 1958, the Soviets launched a dog named Laika. The following year, the United States sent two monkeys, Able and Baker, into space.

 For More Information

BOOKS

Bachrach, Deborah. *The Importance of Margaret Sanger.* San Diego: Lucent Books, 1993.

Baldwin, Joyce. *DNA Pioneer: James Watson and the Double Helix.* New York: Walker and Company, 1994.

Bankston, John. *Francis Crick and James Watson: Pioneers in DNA Research.* Bear, DE: Mitchell Lane Publishers, 2002.

Billings, Charlene W. *Grace Hopper: Navy Admiral and Computer Pioneer.* Hillside, NJ: Enslow Publishers, 1989.

Billings, Charlene W. *Lasers: The New Technology of Light.* New York: Facts on File, 1992.

Boon, Kevin Alexander. *The Human Genome Project: What Does Decoding DNA Mean for Us.* Berkeley Heights, NJ: Enslow Publishers, 2002.

Dash, Joan. *The Triumph of Discovery: Women Scientists Who Won the Nobel Prize.* Englewood Cliffs, NJ: Julian Messner, 1991.

Drieman, J.E. *Atomic Dawn: A Biography of Robert Oppenheimer.* Minneapolis, MN: Dillon Press, 1989.

Dukert, Joseph M. *Nuclear Ships of the World.* New York: Coward, McCann & Geoghegan, 1973.

Edelson, Edward. *Francis Crick and James Watson and the Building Blocks of Life.* New York: Oxford University Press, 1998.

Fridell, Ron. *DNA Fingerprinting: The Ultimate Identity.* New York: Franklin Watts, 2001.

Gardner, Robert. *Health Science Projects About Heredity.* Berkeley Heights, NJ: Enslow Publishers, 2001.

Gonzales, Doreen. *The Manhattan Project and the Atomic Bomb in American History.* Berkeley Heights, NJ: Enslow Publishers, 2000.

Lampton, Christopher. *Wernher von Braun.* New York: Franklin Watts, 1988.

Larsen, Rebecca. *Oppenheimer and the Atomic Bomb.* New York: Franklin Watts, 1988.

Nardo, Don. *Lasers: Humanity's Magic Light.* San Diego: Lucent Books, 1990.

Newton, David E. *James Watson and Francis Crick: Discovery of the Double Helix and Beyond.* New York: Facts on File, 1992.

Northrup, Mary. *American Computer Pioneers.* Springfield, NJ: Enslow Publishers, 1998.

Rummel, Jack. *Robert Oppenheimer: Dark Prince.* New York: Facts on File, 1992.

Senker, Cath. *Rosalind Franklin.* Austin, TX: Raintree Steck-Vaughn, 2002.

Sherrow, Victoria. *James Watson and Francis Crick: Decoding the Secrets of DNA.* Woodbridge, CT: Blackbirch Press, 1995.

Spangenburg, Ray, and Diane K. Moser. *Wernher von Braun: Space Visionary and Rocket Engineer.* New York: Facts on File, 1995.

Thro, Ellen. *Robotics: The Marriage of Computers and Machines.* New York, Facts on File, 1993.

Topalian, Elyse. *Margaret Sanger.* New York: Franklin Watts, 1984.

Whitelaw, Nancy. *Margaret Sanger: "Every Child a Wanted Child."* New York: Dillon Press, 1994.

WEB SITES

Attachment Across Cultures—Research Report. http://www.attachmentcross cultures.org/research/supplement.html (accessed on August 9, 2002).

Biographies: Louis Leakey. http://www.talkorigins.org/faqs/homs/lleakey.html (accessed on August 9, 2002).

History of Space Exploration: Sputnik Satellite Program. http://www.nauts.com/ vehicles/50s/sputnik.html (accessed on August 9, 2002).

Sakharov's H-Bomb. http://www.thebulletin.org/issues/1990/o90/o90bethe.html (accessed on August 9, 2002).

Timeline, 1950. http://hammer.prohosting.com/~penz/computer/time1950.htm (accessed on August 9, 2002).

USAF Museum. http://www.wpafb.af.mil/museum/50th/event50.htm (accessed on August 9, 2002).

chapter eight *Sports*

1950: **January 19–22** The Ladies' Professional Golf Association (LPGA) holds its inaugural tournament.

1950: **April–May** The American Bowling Congress (ABC) ends its white-male-only policy.

1950: **August 8** Florence Chadwick swims the English Channel in thirteen hours and twenty minutes, a women's record.

1950: **August 29** Althea Gibson becomes the first black woman to compete in a national tennis tournament.

1951: **February 14** Sugar Ray Robinson takes the middleweight boxing championship from Jake LaMotta.

1951: **March 2** The National Basketball Association (NBA) holds its first All-Star game.

1951: **April 18** New York Yankees rookie Mickey Mantle makes his major league debut.

1951: **May 25** New York Giants rookie Willie Mays makes his major league debut.

1951: **October 3** Bobby Thomson hits the "Shot Heard 'Round the World," catapulting the New York Giants into the World Series.

1951: **October 10** Joe DiMaggio plays his final game for the New York Yankees.

1952: **April 30** Ted Williams of the Boston Red Sox homers in his final at-bat before heading off to serve in the Marines as a fighter pilot in the Korean War.

1952: **September 23** Rocky Marciano beats Jersey Joe Walcott for the heavyweight championship.

1953: **February 15** Tenley Albright becomes the first American to win the world figure skating title.

1953: **March 18** In the first franchise shift in major league baseball since 1903, the Boston Braves move to Milwaukee.

1953: **July 10** Ben Hogan takes the British Open, after already having won the Masters and the U.S. Open, making him the first golfer ever to win all three major championships in the same year.

1953: **October 5** The New York Yankees become the first team ever to win five consecutive World Series.

1953: **November 9** The U.S. Supreme Court upholds its 1922 ruling that exempts Major League Baseball from antitrust laws.

1954: **April 23** Milwaukee Braves rookie Henry "Hank" Aaron hits the first of his 755 major league home runs.

1954: **August 16** The first issue of *Sports Illustrated* magazine hits the news-stands.

1954: **September 29** Willie Mays's over-the-shoulder catch leads the New York Giants to victory against the Cleveland Indians in the first game of the World Series.

1954: **October** The NBA introduces the twenty-four-second shot clock.

1955: **May 30** Bill Vukovich, winner of the previous two Indianapolis 500s, dies in a crash in this year's race.

1955: **October 4** The Brooklyn Dodgers defeat the New York Yankees in the World Series. It is the franchise's lone championship while in Brooklyn.

1956: **June 29** Charles Dumas becomes the first person to high-jump more than seven feet.

1956: **October 8** New York Yankee Don Larsen pitches a perfect game in the World Series.

1956: **December 13** Jackie Robinson is trad-ed from the Brooklyn Dodgers to the New York Giants. He chooses to retire instead.

1957: **February 25** The U.S. Supreme Court rules that the National Football League (NFL) is not similar to Major League Baseball, and must comply with antitrust laws.

1957: **May 4** Iron Liege wins the Kentucky Derby when jockey Willie Shoemaker, rid-ing Gallant Man, misjudges the finish line.

1957: **September 24** The Brooklyn Dodgers play their final game at Ebbets Field. The following season they relocate to Los Angeles and the New York Giants move to San Francisco.

1957: **November 16** In college football, Notre Dame ends Oklahoma's forty-seven-game winning streak with a 7–0 victory.

1958: **January 12** College football adopts the two-point conversion option fol-lowing a touchdown.

1958: **January 29** Dodgers catcher Roy Campanella is paralyzed in an auto accident.

1958: **December 28** In one of the most sig-nificant games in NFL history, the Bal-timore Colts stun the New York Giants, 23–17, in overtime, and win the league championship.

1959: **May 26** Pittsburgh Pirates hurler Harvey Haddix pitches a perfect game for twelve innings but loses in the thirteenth.

In the 1950s Americans by the millions found more time in which to indulge in leisure activities. However, with the significant exception of bowling adults did not embrace participating in sports. "Playing ball" was considered the exclusive domain of professionals and schoolboys. While boys in grade school played competitive games in schoolyards or Little League, girls usually jumped rope; women with unoccupied hours were encouraged to enhance their cooking or sewing skills rather than their tennis serves or golf swings.

On weekends, men often plopped down on their sofas, turned on their new television sets, and watched sports. By contemporary standards, TV sports were positively medieval. Events were telecast in black and white. There were no instant replays, and camera coverage was distant from the action and severely limited. Because they were easier to televise, the sports that best suited early television were indoor contests such as boxing, wrestling, and roller derby.

Throughout the 1950s, baseball remained America's national pastime. and New York was America's premier baseball town. Back then, three major league teams called New York home: the American League (AL) New York Yankees, which played in Yankee Stadium, located in the Bronx; the National League (NL) Brooklyn Dodgers, whose home field was Brooklyn's Ebbets Field; and the NL New York Giants, who played in Manhattan's Polo Grounds. The Yankees dominated the decade, winning five consecutive World Series between 1949 and 1953; they triumphed again in 1956 and 1958. In total, the so-called Bronx Bombers played in eight of the decade's ten World Series. Their frequent opponents were the Dodgers, who won their first and only title in Brooklyn in 1955. The Giants, meanwhile, lost to the Yankees in 1951 and beat the Cleveland Indians in 1954. After the 1957 season, the Dodgers and Giants shocked and saddened the city's NL fans when they abandoned New York for the orange groves of Los Angeles (the Dodgers' new home) and the bay breezes of San Francisco (where the Giants settled).

In the 1950s, other professional sports were insignificant in comparison to baseball. Yet the decade saw the slow emergence of professional football as a sport that could rivet the nation's attention. One game in particular, a thrilling 1958 championship contest between the National Football League (NFL) New York Giants and Baltimore Colts, was key to the game's maturing. The National Basketball Association (NBA), which came into existence in 1949, was experiencing growing pains. One team, the Minneapolis Lakers, dominated the first part of the decade. Near the end, the Boston Celtics began a dynasty that would last through the following decade. Meanwhile, the National Hockey League (NHL) was a small six-team outfit and was of interest mostly in Canada and in the U.S. cities that hosted NHL franchises.

On the college sports scene, a betting scandal at the dawn of the decade tainted basketball. The Oklahoma Sooners were the era's major college football story; they mounted two impressive winning streaks of thirty-one and forty-seven games. Two Olympics were held; both were focused more on national pride and Cold War politics than competition. The decade saw the rise of the great heavyweight boxing champion Rocky Marciano, who won and defended his title before retiring undefeated. Women athletes, meanwhile, were almost invisible. Yet several earned coverage on the sports pages, including bowling legend Marion Ladewig, tennis stars Maureen "Little Mo" Connolly and Althea Gibson, and all-around athlete Mildred "Babe" Didrikson Zaharias.

Althea Gibson (1927–) During the 1940s, Althea Gibson began winning tennis tournaments that featured black players. Then she set out to break the sport's color line. In 1950, the United States' Lawn Tennis Association (USLTA) allowed her to play in the Nationals. Even though she lost that first match, a barrier had been broken. Over the next few years, Gibson steadily rose in the USLTA rankings. In 1956, she came in first in the French Open in both singles and doubles; then in 1957 and 1958, she won both the U.S. Open and Wimbledon titles. *Photo reproduced by permission of AP/Wide World Photos.*

Ben Hogan (1912–) While golfers like Arnold Palmer, Jack Nicklaus, and Tiger Woods would define the sport in future generations, Ben Hogan was champion of the links during the late 1940s and 1950s. In 1949, he survived a car crash after which doctors predicted that he might not walk, let alone compete as a golfer. Yet he won more than sixty tournaments in his career, many of them after the accident. Hogan enjoyed his greatest success in 1953, when he became the first golfer to win the Masters, the U.S. Open, and the British Open all in the same season. *Photo reproduced by permission of the Corbis Corporation.*

Gordie Howe (1928–) During the 1950s, the Montreal Canadiens and Detroit Red Wings dominated the six-team National Hockey League (NHL). Gordie Howe was the game's reigning superstar. The smooth-skating Howe, who played for the Red Wings, suited up for an amazing thirty-two professional seasons over four decades (1946–71, 1973–80). He led the NHL in scoring on six occasions and was league MVP four times in the 1950s. For twenty-one straight seasons, Howe was among the Top 10 NHL scorers. Howe earned the nickname "Mr. Hockey." *Photo reproduced courtesy of the Library of Congress.*

Mickey Mantle (1931–1995) Mickey Mantle was one of the most mythic baseball stars of the 1950s. Millions idolized him for his athleticism and talent for blasting home runs. Twice he topped fifty homers in a season. He played in twenty All-Star games and, in 1956, Mantle won the Triple Crown by leading the league in home runs, RBIs, and batting average. Unfortunately Mantle suffered through an endless string of ailments; one can only imagine what his statistics might have been if he had not been injured so often. *Photo reproduced by permission of Archive Photos, Inc.*

Willie Mays (1931–) Many believe that Willie Mays, the "Say Hey Kid," was the greatest outfielder in baseball history. Some outfielders primarily are home run hitters, while others are defensive experts. Yet Mays was a specialist in every aspect of the game. He won eleven straight Gold Gloves for his fielding. He led the National League in stolen bases four times. Twice he topped fifty home runs, and he finished his career with 660 four-base hits. Mays's over-the-shoulder catch in Game One of the 1954 World Series is one of the most famous plays in postseason history.

Mildred "Babe" Didrikson Zaharias (1911–1956) Mildred "Babe" Didrikson Zaharias was an amazing athlete. She mastered just about every sport she tried, from basketball and billiards to track-and-field and volleyball. She won two gold medals at the 1932 Olympics, in the javelin throw and 80-meter hurdles, and a silver in the high-jump. During her career, she won fifty-five professional and amateur golf competitions. In 1949, she helped found the Ladies' Professional Golf Association (LPGA) and was U.S. Open champ in 1948, 1950, and 1954. She earned six Women Athlete of the Year awards; in 1950 the Associated Press named her Woman Athlete of the Half-Century. Zaharias was nicknamed "Babe" for the Ruthian home runs she blasted while playing baseball!

◆◆◆◆ *Topics in the News*

❖ INTEGRATED BASEBALL IS DOMINATED BY NEW YORK TEAMS

In 1947, Jackie Robinson (1919–1972) became the first African American to play major league baseball in the twentieth century. Other black players followed, with their numbers slowly increasing during the 1950s. Yet most rosters remained predominantly white and some were completely segregated. In mid-July 1959, the Boston Red Sox became the final major league club to employ a black ballplayer by bringing to the majors infielder Pumpsie Green (1933–). Despite the slow pace of integration, quite a few of baseball's rising stars were black. Among them were Willie Mays, Henry "Hank" Aaron, Frank Robinson, Ernie Banks, Minnie Minoso, Don Newcombe, and Jim Gilliam. Had they been born a couple of decades earlier, all would have missed playing in the major leagues solely because of the color of their skin.

The American League (AL) New York Yankees were the kings of baseball in the 1950s. Their skipper throughout the decade was Casey Stengel (1890–1975), a former National League (NL) outfielder who during the 1930s and 1940s managed the lowly Brooklyn Dodgers and Boston Braves. Given his track record, his elevation to the Yankees stewardship in 1949 was surprising. However, Stengel brilliantly platooned his players and juggled his line ups. During the next twelve seasons, he won ten pennants and seven world championships.

After the 1951 season, Joe DiMaggio (1914–1999), the Bronx Bombers' legendary centerfielder, retired. He promptly was replaced by another all-time Yankee great, Mickey Mantle (1931–1995). In 1956, Mantle won the Triple Crown, leading the AL in batting average (.353), runs-batted-in (130), and home runs (52). Between 1949 and 1953, the Yankees won an astonishing five straight World Series. They won again in 1956 and 1958, and lost in 1955 (to the Brooklyn Dodgers) and 1957 (to the Milwaukee Braves). Only twice during the decade, in 1954 and 1959, did they not play in the Series. Of all Yankees World Series contests throughout the decade, easily the most memorable was Game Five of the '56 series. Don Larsen (1929–), an otherwise average pitcher who finished his career with a losing record, pitched a perfect game. Larsen faced the minimum twenty-seven batters and retired every one of them.

*OPPOSITE PAGE
Willie Mays was one of baseball's rising African American stars during the 1950s. Reproduced by permission of AP/Wide World Photos.*

The Yankees were not the only New York team to find success during the 1950s. In fact, the late 1940s through mid-1950s was a golden era for all New York baseball fans. The New York Giants played in the World

Major League Baseball World Series

Year	Winning Team	Losing Team
1950	New York Yankees (AL) 4	Philadelphia Phillies (NL) 0
1951	New York Yankees (AL) 4	New York Giants (NL) 2
1952	New York Yankees (AL) 4	Brooklyn Dodgers (NL) 3
1953	New York Yankees (AL) 4	Brooklyn Dodgers (NL) 2
1954	New York Giants (NL) 4	Cleveland Indians (AL) 0
1955	Brooklyn Dodgers (NL) 4	New York Yankees (AL) 3
1956	New York Yankees (AL) 4	Brooklyn Dodgers (NL) 3
1957	Milwaukee Braves (NL) 4	New York Yankees (AL) 3
1958	New York Yankees (AL) 4	Milwaukee Braves (NL) 3
1959	Los Angeles Dodgers (NL) 4	Chicago White Sox (AL) 2

Series in 1951 and 1954, while the Brooklyn Dodgers did so in 1947, 1949, 1952, 1953, 1955, and 1956. In each of their series, the Dodgers opposed the mighty Yankees. Each year, they were defeated by their uptown rivals, leading Brooklyn loyalists to chant a phrase that came to symbolize their frustration: "Wait 'til next year." "Next year" finally arrived in 1955, when the Dodgers (who fondly were known as "Dem Bums") beat the Yankees in a seven-game series. In the deciding contest, pitcher Johnny Podres (1932–) quieted the Yankees' bats, shutting them out 2 to 0. It was the lone world championship won by the Dodgers while the franchise was located in Brooklyn.

Meanwhile, Giants rooters savored two memorable baseball moments. In 1951 their team tied the Dodgers for first place with a frantic late-season surge. Each finished with a 96 and 58 record. In the final game of a best-of-three playoff, the Giants' Bobby Thomson (1923–) smacked a dramatic ninth-inning home run off the Dodgers' Ralph Branca (1926–) to hand his team the pennant. The hit, one of the most celebrated in baseball history, came to be known as the "Shot Heard 'Round the World." While the Giants fell four games to two to the Yankees in the 1951 World Series, they came back three years later to sweep the Cleveland Indians, who during the regular season had won a then-record 111 games. The defining moment of that series came in Game One. With the score knotted at 2 to 2 in the

Bill Veeck (pronounced VECK; 1914–1986), major league baseball owner, was a maverick and an innovator. He integrated the American League (in 1947, when he owned the Cleveland Indians), placed players' names on the backs of their uniforms, and invented the "exploding" scoreboard with fireworks and sounds.

Occasionally, however, a Veeck prank could be downright goofy. In 1951, he owned the lowly St. Louis Browns. That August, he signed Eddie Gaedel (1925–1961) to a professional contract. What made this pact so unusual was that Gaedel was just three-feet-seven-inches tall! Gaedel was assigned uniform number 1/8. In the first inning of an August game against the Detroit Tigers, Gaedel came up to bat. He was walked on four pitches, and pulled for a pinch runner.

Not surprisingly, several days later Veeck was barred from further employing Gaedel as a major-league ballplayer.

eighth inning, two Indians reached base. Up came Vic Wertz (1925–1983), whose first-inning triple had given the Indians a 2 to 0 lead. Wertz smashed a fly ball that, had the game been played in Cleveland, would have been a home run. Instead, it was nothing more than a 425-foot out, as Giants centerfielder Willie Mays (1931–) raced back and made a dramatic, over-the-shoulder catch. Mays's catch is arguably the most famous in World Series history. A three-run ninth-inning home run by pinch hitter Dusty Rhodes (1927–) won the game for the Giants. (Throughout the decade, New York sports fans relished debating which team sported the best centerfielder: Mays, Mantle, or the Dodgers' Duke Snider [1926–)].)

While New York teams ruled baseball, the decade concluded on a somber note for many of the city's fans. At the end of the 1957 season, the Dodgers and Giants abandoned their roots, relocating respectively to Los Angeles and San Francisco. In 1959, Ebbets Field, the Dodgers' ballpark, was torn down and replaced by a housing project. It is remembered to this day as one of baseball's most beloved stadiums. The Polo Grounds, the Giants' ballpark, lasted into the 1960s. In 1962, the NL added two expansion teams, the Houston Colt .45s (later renamed the Astros) and the New York Mets. Before moving into newly constructed Shea Stadium in 1964, the Mets played two seasons in the Polo Grounds. Then it, too, fell victim to the wrecking ball.

The Dodgers and Giants were not the only major league franchises to shift cities during the decade. In consecutive seasons beginning in 1953, the Boston Braves switched to Milwaukee, the St. Louis Browns became the Baltimore Orioles, and the Philadelphia Athletics moved to Kansas City.

❖ COLLEGE BASKETBALL'S TARNISHED IMAGE

The 1950s began with one of the more shameful scandals in college sports history. In 1951, the New York district attorney's office announced that it had uncovered evidence that basketball players at many of the nation's top schools were "shaving points" (not playing to their full capabilities). In exchange, they were being paid off by gamblers. Reportedly, gamblers had approached the players while they were spending their summers playing at resorts in upstate New York's Catskill Mountains.

Among the culprits were stars of the City College of New York (CCNY) team. Incredibly, CCNY had won both the National Invitation Tournament (NIT) and National Collegiate Athletic Association (NCAA) championship in 1950. Players from New York University (NYU), Long Island University (LIU), Manhattan, Toledo, Kentucky, and Bradley also were implicated. They were called to testify before grand juries, and the image of college basketball was tarnished for the rest of the decade.

Despite the scandal, the 1950s did see its share of great college basketball teams and players. For example, the University of San Francisco, led by future Boston Celtics legends Bill Russell (1934–) and K. C. Jones (1931–), won NCAA championships in 1955 and 1956. Kentucky was also a consistent national power, winning NCAA titles in 1949, 1951, and 1958.

❖ PROFESSIONAL BASKETBALL TAKES HOLD

In 1949, two existing professional leagues—the Basketball Association of America (BAA) and National Basketball League (NBL)—combined to become the most profitable and stable of all pro leagues: The National Basketball Association (NBA). However, during the decade, the NBA had not yet evolved into a high-profile, world-renowned league. It still was a jumble of teams, many of which were financially shaky and noncompetitive.

Three years before the NBA officially began, the BAA was comprised of eleven teams: the Boston Celtics; Chicago Stags; Cleveland Rebels; Detroit Falcons; New York Knickerbockers; Philadelphia Warriors; Pittsburgh Ironmen; Providence Steamrollers; St. Louis Bombers; Toronto Huskies;

NCAA Division I Men's Basketball Champions

1950:	City College of New York
1951:	Kentucky
1952:	Kansas
1953:	Indiana
1954:	La Salle
1955:	San Francisco
1956:	San Francisco
1957:	North Carolina
1958:	Kentucky
1959:	California

and Washington Capitals. In 1947, the Baltimore Bullets joined the BAA, while four franchises (Cleveland, Detroit, Pittsburgh, and Toronto) ceased operations. The following year, four NBL teams were added to the BAA: the Fort Wayne (Indiana) Pistons, Indianapolis Jets, Minneapolis Lakers, and Rochester (New York) Royals. The remaining NBL teams were the Anderson (Indiana) Packers; Denver Nuggets; Indianapolis Olympians; Sheboygan (Wisconsin) Redskins; Syracuse Nationals; Tri-Cities Blackhawks (which played its home games in Moline and Rock Island, Illinois, and Davenport, Iowa); and Waterloo (Indiana) Hawks. They, plus the new Indianapolis Olympians, joined the BAA, which later became the NBA.

In 1949, Providence and Indianapolis disbanded, leaving the NBA with seventeen teams divided into three divisions. Then in 1950, six teams left: Anderson, Chicago, Denver, Sheboygan, St. Louis, and Waterloo. They were followed by Washington in 1951, Indianapolis in 1953, and Baltimore in 1954. Additionally, there were franchise shifts in which teams switched cities, and sometimes names as well. In 1951, the Tri-Cities Blackhawks became the Milwaukee Hawks. In 1955, the Hawks moved to St. Louis. In 1957, the Fort Wayne Pistons shifted to Detroit and the Rochester Royals headed for Cincinnati. By the end of the decade, the NBA consisted of eight teams separated into two divisions.

The Minneapolis (later Los Angeles) Lakers were the decade's leading NBA team, winning four league championships. They were coached by

NBA Championships

Year	Winning Team	Losing Team
1950	Minneapolis Lakers, 4	Syracuse Nationals, 3
1951	Rochester Royals, 4	New York Knicks, 3
1952	Minneapolis Lakers, 4	New York Knicks, 3
1953	Minneapolis Lakers, 4	New York Knicks, 1
1954	Minneapolis Lakers, 4	Syracuse Nationals, 3
1955	Syracuse Nationals, 4	Fort Wayne Pistons, 3
1956	Philadelphia Warriors, 4	Fort Wayne Pistons, 1
1957	Boston Celtics, 4	Saint Louis Hawks, 3
1958	Saint Louis Hawks, 4	Boston Celtics, 2
1959	Boston Celtics, 4	Minneapolis Lakers, 0

John Kundla and led by players George Mikan, Jim Pollard, Slater Martin, and Vern Mikkelson. Yet during the decade, the NBA was a secondary sports league. Its top players were not as celebrated as the stars of baseball and even football. Contests frequently were awkward and boring, ruled by slow-footed big men and stretched out by endless fouling aimed at impeding fast breaks.

To add vitality to NBA contests, the league instituted rule adjustments to make the game faster and more high-scoring. Then in 1957, the Boston Celtics, under coach Arnold "Red" Auerbach (1917–), won its first NBA championship. After a playoff defeat to St. Louis the following season, the Celts earned an amazing eight straight league titles.

❖ BOWLING: THE PEOPLE'S SPORT

During the 1950s, bowling was the country's most popular participation sport. The advent of automatic pin-setting machines and more stable wood oils made the game popular and easier to play. Bowling alleys sprouted up across the nation and Americans by the thousands entered local leagues, whose numbers peaked during the mid-1960s. Tournaments were televised locally and nationally. Handicap tournaments allowed lesser bowlers an advantage computed on the basis of previous performances.

1949–51:	Ezzard Charles
1951–52:	Jersey Joe Walcott
1952–56:	Rocky Marciano
1956–59:	Floyd Patterson
1959–60:	Ingemar Johansson

Thus, average players could battle professionals. Truly, bowling was a sport of the masses, enjoyed by everyday working people.

Bowling was also sport enjoyed by both men and women. While local competitive leagues were available for each gender, there were coed recreational leagues as well. Among professionals, Marion Ladewig (1914–) was queen of the lanes. She began bowling in 1937, and retired as a pro in 1964. In between, she won dozens of tournaments. On eight occasions in the 1950s, the Bowling Writers' Association of America (BWAA) named her Bowler of the Year.

❖ MARCIANO AND ROBINSON DOMINATE BOXING

From 1937 through the end of the 1940s, Joe Louis (1914–1981), the Brown Bomber, reigned as world heavyweight champion. During the early post-Louis era, no single fighter with his toughness and talent came forward. Ezzard Charles (1921–1975) and Jersey Joe Walcott (1914–1994) fought three times for the title, but neither had the power and savvy that had made Louis the greatest boxer since Jack Dempsey (1895–1983) during the 1920s.

Then came one of the all-time top heavyweights: Rocky Marciano (1923–1969), who took the title from Walcott in 1952. A year earlier, he had knocked out Louis, who was unsuccessfully attempting a comeback. Marciano went on to compile a perfect 49 and 0 record, which included 43 KOs (knock-outs). He retired undefeated in 1956. Floyd Patterson (1935–), who won a gold medal at the 1952 Olympics as a middleweight, followed Marciano as heavyweight champ. He lost the title in 1959 to Ingemar Johansson (1932–) and became the first boxer to regain it when he beat Johansson the following year.

Rocky Marciano may have been the top heavyweight of the 1950s, but some boxing aficionados argue that, pound for pound, Sugar Ray Robinson (1921–1989) was the decade's greatest fighter. Robinson was fabled for his lightning speed, rocklike toughness, and devastating punching

power. In 1951, he took the middleweight title from Jake LaMotta (1921–); it was the last of six classic battles between the two. Before the decade ended, Robinson lost and regained the crown four more times.

❖ PRO FOOTBALL COMES OF AGE

The National Football League (NFL) had been in existence since the early 1920s. Yet three decades later, it lacked the wide popularity it would come to enjoy in the future. Nonetheless, the decade saw the sport steadily grow and attract increasing numbers of fans, until it surpassed college football in popularity.

The 1950s did see its share of college grid greats. One of the decade's most unusual accomplishments came in 1956, when Notre Dame's Paul Hornung (1935–), the "Golden Boy," won the Heisman Trophy despite playing for a losing team. That year, the Fighting Irish were 2 and 8! Coach Bud Wilkinson (1916–1994) led Oklahoma to three national titles (in 1950, 1955, and 1956), and four Orange Bowl and two Sugar Bowl victories. Between 1948 and 1950 and 1953 and 1957, the Sooners mounted winning streaks of thirty-one and forty-seven straight games.

However, the football story of the decade was the emergence of the NFL. In 1950, it was a thirteen-team league divided into two divisions. It expanded that year, adding three teams—the Cleveland Browns, San Francisco 49ers, and Baltimore Colts—from the rival All-America Football Conference (AAFC), which had just folded. The Browns and Detroit Lions dominated the first half of the decade, with Cleveland winning NFL titles in 1950, 1954, and 1955 and Detroit triumphing in 1952, 1953, and 1957. (The Super Bowl would not come into being until the 1960s.) To start its inaugural NFL season, Cleveland took on the heavily favored Philadelphia Eagles (which had won the final two league championships during the 1940s). Yet the Browns prevailed, 35 to 10, with quarterback Otto Graham (1921–) picking apart the Eagle defense as he completed twenty-one passes for 346 yards. Cleveland capped its NFL debut with a 30 to 28 victory over the Los Angeles Rams in the championship contest. Browns' placekicker Lou Groza (1924–2000) won it by booting a 28-yard field goal with twenty-eight seconds left on the clock.

Despite these heroics, the one NFL game that had the most impact on the league's growth was the 1958 championship. That year, the New York Giants and Baltimore Colts met in front of a record number of television viewers. On the final day of the regular season, the Cleveland Browns held a one-game edge over New York. The two teams faced off and, on the game's first play, Cleveland fullback Jim Brown (1936–) ran 65 yards for a

OPPOSITE PAGE
Rocky Marciano was the heavyweight boxing champion during most of the 1950s.
Reproduced by permission of AP/Wide World Photos

NFL Championships

Year	Winning Team	Losing Team
1950	Cleveland Browns, 30	Los Angeles Rams, 28
1951	Los Angeles Rams, 24	Cleveland Browns, 17
1952	Detroit Lions, 17	Cleveland Browns, 7
1953	Detroit Lions, 17	Cleveland Browns, 16
1954	Cleveland Browns, 46	Detroit Lions, 10
1955	Cleveland Browns, 28	Los Angeles Rams, 14
1956	New York Giants, 47	Chicago Bears, 7
1957	Detroit Lions, 59	Cleveland Browns, 14
1958	Baltimore Colts, 23	New York Giants, 17
1959	Baltimore Colts, 31	New York Giants, 16

touchdown. But Cleveland lost, 13 to 10, as Giants place-kicker Pat Summerall (1930–) booted a 49-yard field goal through the wind and snow that had enveloped Yankee Stadium. The Giants prevailed, 10 to 0, in a one-game playoff, and took on the Colts for the title. With two minutes left to play and the Colts down by a touchdown, quarterback Johnny Unitas (1933–2002) led his team 73 yards downfield. With seven seconds to play, Steve Myhra (1934–1994) kicked a 20-yard field goal, tying the game at 17 to 17 and sending it into overtime. Eight minutes and fifteen seconds later, in what might be the most celebrated scoring play in NFL history, Baltimore fullback Alan Ameche (1933–1988) rushed one yard for the winning touchdown. Television viewers were dazzled not only by the thrilling climax but also by Unitas's precision passing during the pivotal fourth-quarter scoring drive.

The 1950s saw many NFL legends grinding out gridiron yardage and tossing or catching passes. The great Detroit teams were sparked by quarterback Bobby Layne, halfback Doak Walker, linebacker Joe Schmidt, and defensive backs Jack Christiansen and Yale Lary. In mid-decade, the New York Giants became a force with its strong defense, sparked by ends Andy Robustelli and Jim Katcavage, tackles Dick Modzelewski and Roosevelt Grier, and middle linebacker Sam Huff. The Baltimore Colts were led by Unitas, end Raymond Berry, halfback Lenny Moore, tackle Jim Parker, and defensive linemen Art Donovan and Gino Marchetti. A string of great quarterbacks played during the decade, including Bob Waterfield, Norm Van Brocklin, Charlie Conerly, Y.A. Tittle, Unitas, Layne, and Graham.

❖ POLITICS IN THE OLYMPICS

While the Olympic Games are supposed to spotlight international athletes in a nonpolitical setting, this often is not the case. As the cold war (a war of ideas and political systems between the United States and Russia and their respective allies) raged during the 1950s, the Olympics often became a test of superiority between East and West.

East-West tensions were apparent at the 1952 games in Helsinki, Finland, where the Soviets refused to house their athletes in the Olympic Village. Instead, competitors representing Russia and its satellite nations stayed in separate quarters surrounded by barbed wire! Meanwhile, Nationalist China, the leadership of which had fled to the island of Taiwan after being defeated by Communist leaders in 1948, claimed to be the lone official Chinese team. Initially, the International Olympic Organizing Committee (IOC) declared that neither Nationalist nor Communist (mainland) China could compete, but then changed its policy and invited both. Then Nationalist China boycotted the games. East Germany was barred from competition because there was not yet international recognition of it as a country. Political fallout extended to athletes who had no country of citizenship because their homelands still were fragmented as a result of World War II. They petitioned to compete under the Olympic, Swiss, Greek, or Red Cross flags. The IOC ignored their requests.

The 1956 games in Melbourne, Australia, were no less contentious. Spain, Switzerland, and The Netherlands boycotted in protest of the Soviet invasion of Hungary. Communist China withdrew because Nationalist China had been invited. Egypt withdrew because it was at war with Israel. Iraq withdrew because of military action several nations had taken against Egypt in the struggle for control of the Suez Canal. Norway requested that the IOC bar South Africa because of its racial policies. Once the games had begun, politically allied nations frequently accused judges of favoritism. Politics further spilled onto the playing field when Russia and Hungary met in a semifinal water polo match which ended in a bloody fight.

❖ SPORTS ON TV, STAGE, AND SCREEN

With the steadily rising popularity of television, sports programming quickly became a natural ratings booster. It was inexpensive to produce, it could be sold to the public with a minimum of marketing, and it provided

Americans with yet one more reason to purchase TV sets. Early in the decade, boxing, wrestling, and roller derby brought plenty of action to sports aficionados. As the years passed, all types of sports were broadcast with increased frequency. By 1958, more than eight hundred baseball games were telecast regionally and nationally. However, there were no instant replays, no color, few close-ups, and limited camera coverage. Transmissions frequently were interrupted by technical glitches.

Boxing broadcasts in particular had a major effect on the then-escalating popularity of television. In 1949, Jimmy Powers (1903–1995), a New York *Daily News* sports editor and columnist, became the key announcer on the *Gillette Cavalcade of Sports* (1948–1960). He was at ringside for what became popularly known as the "Friday Night Fights," describing the action to boxing fans crowded around TV sets at home or in neighborhood bars.

During the 1950s, Americans craved heroes. To fill this need, Hollywood studios produced a string of movies spotlighting the fictionalized stories of real-life athletes. Usually, they charted how their main characters triumphed over hardship and won glory on the playing field.

The decade's sports biography films included *The Jackie Robinson Story* (1950), in which Robinson starred as himself; *Follow the Sun* (1951), with Glenn Ford as golfer Ben Hogan; *Jim Thorpe: All American* (1951), starring Burt Lancaster as the Olympic legend; *The Pride of St. Louis* (1952) and *The Winning Team* (1952), respectively featuring Dan Dailey and future U.S. president Ronald Reagan as hall-of-fame pitchers Dizzy Dean and Grover Cleveland Alexander; *The Joe Louis Story* (1953), with Coley Wallace as the heavyweight champion; *Crazylegs* (1953), featuring football star Elroy "Crazylegs" Hirsch as himself; *The Bob Mathias Story* (1954), with Olympic star Mathias playing himself; *Somebody Up There Likes Me* (1956), with Paul Newman as boxer Rocky Graziano; and *Fear Strikes Out* (1957), featuring Anthony Perkins as baseball player Jimmy Piersall. The story of the Harlem Globetrotters, the celebrated barnstorming basketball team, was recounted in *The Harlem Globetrotters* (1951) and *Go, Man, Go!* (1954).

During the 1950s, baseball's New York Yankees were so powerful that one of the era's clichés was that supporting them was the equivalent of rooting for U.S. Steel (the richest and most powerful American company of the day). In 1955, Yankee-bashing even reached Broadway when the musical *Damn Yankees* opened on Broadway. *Damn Yankees* was the story of a die-hard Washington Senators fan who barters his soul to the devil to have his team beat the dreaded Yankees. It was made into a film three years later.

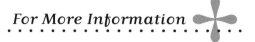
BOOKS

Aaron, Hank, with Dick Schaap. *Home Run: My Life in Pictures*. Kingston, NY: Total Sports, 1999.

Allen, Maury. *Big-Time Baseball: A Complete Record of the National Sport*. New York: Hart Publishing Company, 1978.

Bacho, Peter. *Boxing in Black and White*. New York: Henry Holt, 1999.

Biracree, Tom. *Althea Gibson*. New York: Chelsea House, 1989.

Carrieri, Joe. *Joe DiMaggio: The Promise*. Mineola, NY: Carlyn Publications, 2000.

Carroll, Bob, Michael Gershman, David Neff, and John Thorn, eds. *Total Football II*. New York: HarperCollins, 1999.

Cayleff, Susan. *Babe Didrikson: The Greatest All-Sport Athlete of All Time*. Berkeley, CA: Conari Press, 2000.

Collins, Bud, and Zander Hollander, eds. *Bud Collins' Modern Encyclopedia of Tennis, Second Edition*. Detroit: Visible Ink Press, 1993.

Coombs, Karen Mueller. *Jackie Robinson: Baseball's Civil Rights Legend*. Springfield, NJ: Enslow Publishers, 1997.

Christopher, Matt. *Great Moments in Baseball History*. Boston: Little, Brown & Company, 1996.

Davidson, Sue. *Changing the Game: The Inside Stories of Tennis Champions Althea Gibson and Alice Marble*. Seattle, WA: Seal Press, 1997.

Diamond, Dan, Ralph Dinger, and James Duplacey, eds. *Total Hockey*. Kingston, NY: Total Sports, 1998.

Edelman, Rob. *Great Baseball Films*. New York: Citadel Press, 1994.

Falla, Jack, ed. *Quest for the Cup: A History of the Stanley Cup Finals, 1893–2001*. San Diego: Thunder Bay Press, 2001.

Flink, Steven. *The Greatest Tennis Matches of the Twentieth Century*. Danbury, CT: Rutledge Books, 1999.

Freedman, Russell. *Babe Didrikson Zaharias: The Making of a Champion*. New York: Clarion Books, 1999.

Gilbert, Thomas. *Damn Yankees: Casey, Whitey, Yogi, and the Mick*. New York: Franklin Watts, 1997.

Greenspan, Bud. *100 Greatest Moments in Olympic History*. Los Angeles: General Publishing Group, 1995.

Heinz, W. C., and Nathan Ward, eds. *The Book of Boxing*. New York: Total Sports, 1999.

Hubbard, Jan, ed. *The Official NBA Encyclopedia, Third Edition*. New York: Doubleday, 2000.

Lynn, Elizabeth. *Babe Didrikson Zaharias*. New York: Chelsea House, 1989.

Macht, Norman L. *Roy Campanella: Baseball Star.* New York: Chelsea House, 1996.

Mays, Willie, with Lou Sahadi. *Say Hey: The Autobiography of Willie Mays.* New York: Simon & Schuster, 1988.

Ritter, Lawrence. *The Story of Baseball Rev. ed.* New York: Morrow Junior Books, 1999.

Stewart, Mark. *Baseball: A History of the National Pastime.* New York: Franklin Watts, 1998.

Stewart, Mark. *Basketball: A History of Hoops.* New York: Franklin Watts, 1999.

Stewart, Mark. *Football: A History of the Gridiron Game.* New York: Franklin Watts, 1998.

Thorn, John, Pete Palmer, and Michael Gershman, eds. *Total Baseball,* Kingston, NY: Total Sports, 2001.

Wakeman, Nancy. *Babe Didrikson Zaharias: Driven to Win.* Minneapolis, MN: Lerner Publications, 2000.

Whittingham, Richard. *Rites of Autumn: The Story of College Football.* New York: Free Press, 2001.

Williams, Ted, with David Pietrusza. *Ted Williams: My Life in Pictures.* Kingston, NY: Total Sports, 2001.

WEB SITES

Boxing on TV. http://www.skypoint.com/members/schutz19/boxing.htm (accessed on August 9, 2002).

Major League Baseball Historical Standings 1950s. http://www.fortunecity.com/olympia/zatopek/91/1950s.html (accessed on August 9, 2002).

Pro Football Hall of Fame—History. http://www.profootballhof.com/history/mainpage.cfm?cont_id=113955 (accessed on August 9, 2002).

Where to Learn More

BOOKS

Aaron, Hank, with Dick Schaap. *Home Run: My Life in Pictures.* Kingston, NY: Total Sports, 1999.

Aaseng, Nathan. *More With Less: The Future World of Buckminster Fuller.* Minneapolis: Lerner Publications, 1986.

Allen, Maury. *Big-Time Baseball: A Complete Record of the National Sport.* New York: Hart Publishing Company, 1978.

Allen, Zita. *Black Women Leaders of the Civil Rights Movement.* New York: Franklin Watts, 1996.

Alonso, Karen. *The Alger Hiss Communist Spy Trial: A Headline Court Case.* Berkeley Heights, NJ: Enslow Publishers, 2001.

Andrews, Bart. *The 'I Love Lucy' Book.* Garden City, NY: Doubleday, 1985.

Archer, Jules. *They Had a Dream: The Civil Rights Struggle from Frederick Douglas to Marcus Garvey to Martin Luther King, Jr. and Malcolm X.* New York: Viking, 1993.

Aronson, Marc. *Art Attack: A Short Cultural History of the Avant-Garde.* New York: Clarion Books, 1998.

Bacho, Peter. *Boxing in Black and White.* New York: Henry Holt, 1999.

Bachrach, Deborah. *The Importance of Margaret Sanger.* San Diego: Lucent Books, 1993.

Baker, Patricia. *Fashions of a Decade: The 1950s.* New York: Facts on File, 1991.

Baldwin, Joyce. *DNA Pioneer: James Watson and the Double Helix.* New York: Walker and Company, 1994.

Banfield, Susan. *The Fifteenth Amendment: African-American Men's Right to Vote.* Springfield, NJ: Enslow Publishers, 1998.

Bankston, John. *Francis Crick and James Watson: Pioneers in DNA Research.* Bear, DE: Mitchell Lane Publishers, 2002.

Benson, Sonia G. *Korean War: Biographies.* Farmington Hills, MI: U•X•L, 2001.

Bergamini, Andrea. *The History of Rock Music.* Hauppauge, NY: Barron's, 2000.

Berke, Sally. *When TV Began: The First TV Shows.* New York: CPI, 1978.

Billings, Charlene W. *Grace Hopper: Navy Admiral and Computer Pioneer.* Hillside, NJ: Enslow Publishers, 1989.

Billings, Charlene W. *Lasers: The New Technology of Light.* New York: Facts on File, 1992.

Biracree, Tom. *Althea Gibson.* New York: Chelsea House, 1989.

Boon, Kevin Alexander. *The Human Genome Project: What Does Decoding DNA Mean for Us.* Berkeley Heights, NJ: Enslow Publishers, 2002.

Boulton, Alexander O. *Frank Lloyd Wright, Architect: An Illustrated Biography.* New York: Rizzoli, 1993.

Brinkley, Douglas. *Rosa Parks.* New York: Viking Press, 2000.

Brooks, Tim, and Earle Marsh. *The Complete Directory to Prime Time Network and Cable TV Shows,* 4th ed. New York: Ballantine Books, 1999.

Brooks, Tim. *The Complete Dictionary of Prime Time TV Stars.* New York: Ballantine Books, 1987.

Calabro, Marian. *Zap!: A Brief History of Television.* New York: Maxwell Macmillan International, 1992.

Carrieri, Joe. *Joe DiMaggio: The Promise.* Mineola, NY: Carlyn Publications, 2000.

Carroll, Bob, Michael Gershman, David Neff, and John Thorn, eds. *Total Football II.* New York: HarperCollins, 1999.

Cayleff, Susan. *Babe Didrikson: The Greatest All-Sport Athlete of All Time.* Berkeley, CA: Conari Press, 2000.

Christopher, Matt. *Great Moments in Baseball History.* Boston: Little Brown & Company, 1996.

Clifford, Mike, consultant. *The Illustrated History of Black Music.* New York: Harmony Books, 1982.

Cohen, Daniel. *Joseph McCarthy: The Misuse of Political Power.* Brookfield, CT: Millbrook Press, 1996.

Collins, Bud, and Zander Hollander, eds. *Bud Collins' Modern Encyclopedia of Tennis,* 2nd ed. Detroit: Visible Ink Press, 1993.

Coombs, Karen Mueller. *Jackie Robinson: Baseball's Civil Rights Legend.* Springfield, NJ: Enslow Publishers, 1997.

Daily, Robert. *Elvis Presley: The King of Rock 'n' Roll.* New York: Franklin Watts, 1996.

Dash, Joan. *The Triumph of Discovery: Women Scientists Who Won the Nobel Prize.* Englewood Cliffs, NJ: Julian Messner, 1991.

Davidson, Sue. *Changing the Game: The Inside Stories of Tennis Champions Althea Gibson and Alice Marble.* Seattle, WA: Seal Press, 1997.

Davis, Frances A. *Frank Lloyd Wright: Maverick Architect.* Minneapolis, MN: Lerner Publications, 1996.

Day, Nancy. *Advertising: Information or Manipulation?* Springfield, NJ: Enslow Publishers, 1999.

Deitch, Kenneth M. and JoAnne B. Weisman. *Dwight D. Eisenhower: Man of Many Hats.* Lowell, MA: Discovery Enterprises, 1990.

Denenberg, Barry. *All Shook Up! The Life and Death of Elvis Presley.* New York: Scholastic Press, 2001.

Denenberg, Barry. *The True Story of J. Edgar Hoover and the FBI.* New York: Scholastic Paperbacks, 1995.

Diamond, Dan, Ralph Dinger, and James Duplacey, eds. *Total Hockey.* Kingston, NY: Total Sports, 1998.

Drieman, J. E. *Atomic Dawn: A Biography of Robert Oppenheimer.* Minneapolis: Dillon Press, 1989.

Dubovoy, Sina. *Civil Rights Leaders.* New York; Facts on File, 1997.

Dukert, Joseph M. *Nuclear Ships of the World.* New York: Coward, McCann & Geoghegan, 1973.

Edelman, Rob. *Great Baseball Films.* New York: Citadel Press, 1994.

Edelson, Edward. *Francis Crick and James Watson and the Building Blocks of Life.* New York: Oxford University Press, 1998.

Epstein, Dan. *The 50s.* Broomall, PA: Chelsea House, 2000.

Falkenburg, Claudia, and Andrew Solt. *A Really Big Show: A Visual History of the Ed Sullivan Show.* New York: Viking Studio Books, 1992.

Falla, Jack, ed. *Quest for the Cup: A History of the Stanley Cup Finals, 1893–2001.* San Diego: Thunder Bay Press, 2001.

Farish, Leah. *The First Amendment: Freedom of Speech, Religion, and the Press.* Springfield, NJ: Enslow Publishers, 1998.

Feinberg, Barbara Silberdick. *America's First Ladies: Changing Expectations.* New York: Franklin Watts, 1998.

Feinstein, Stephen. *The 1950s from the Korean War to Elvis.* Berkeley Heights, NJ: Enslow Publishers, 2000.

Fidelman, Geoffrey Mark. *The Lucy Book.* Los Angeles: Renaissance Books, 1999.

Finkelstein, Norman H. *With Heroic Truth: The Life of Edward R. Murrow.* New York: Clarion Books, 1997.

Fireside, Harvey, and Sarah Betsy Fuller. *Brown v. Board of Education: Equal Schooling for All.* Hillside, NJ: Enslow Publishers, 1994.

Fireside, Harvey. *Plessy v. Ferguson: Separate But Equal?* Hillside, NJ: Enslow Publishers, 1997.

Flink, Steven. *The Greatest Tennis Matches of the Twentieth Century.* Danbury, CT: Rutledge Books, 1999.

Freedman, Russell. *Babe Didrikson Zaharias: The Making of a Champion.* New York: Clarion Books, 1999.

Fridell, Ron. *DNA Fingerprinting: The Ultimate Identity.* New York: Franklin Watts, 2001.

Gaines, Ann Graham. *Douglas MacArthur: Brilliant General, Controversial Leader.* Berkeley Heights, NJ: Enslow Publishers, 2001.

Gardner, Robert. *Health Science Projects About Heredity.* Berkeley Heights, NJ: Enslow Publishers, 2001.

Gay, Kathlyn. *Who's Running the Nation? How Corporate Power Threatens Democracy.* New York: Franklin Watts, 1998.

Gilbert, Thomas. *Damn Yankees: Casey, Whitey, Yogi, and the Mick.* New York: Franklin Watts, 1997.

Goldman, Martin S. *Richard M. Nixon: The Complex President.* New York: Facts on File, 1998.

Gonzales, Doreen. *The Manhattan Project and the Atomic Bomb in American History.* Berkeley Heights, NJ: Enslow Publishers, 2000.

Gourley, Catherine. *Media Wizards: A Behind-the-Scenes Look at Media Manipulations.* Brookfield, CT: Twenty-First Century Books, 1999.

Gourse, Leslie. *Blowing on the Changes: The Art of the Jazz Horn Players.* New York: Franklin Watts, 1997.

Greenberg, Cara. *Mid-Century Modern: Furniture of the 1950s.* New York: Harmony Books, 1995.

Greenspan, Bud. *100 Greatest Moments in Olympic History.* Los Angeles: General Publishing Group, 1995.

Halliwell, Sarah, ed. *The 20th Century: Post-1945 Artists, Writers, and Composers.* Austin, TX: Raintree/Steck-Vaughn, 1998.

Haskins, James. *Separate, but Not Equal: The Dream and the Struggle.* New York: Scholastic, 1998.

Hay, Jeff, ed. *Richard Nixon.* San Diego: Greenhaven Press, 2001.

Heinz, W. C., and Nathan Ward, eds. *The Book of Boxing.* New York: Total Sports, 1999.

Herda, D. J. *Earl Warren: Chief Justice for Social Change.* Springfield, NJ: Enslow Publishers, 1995.

Herda, D. J. *Thurgood Marshall: Civil Rights Champion.* Springfield, NJ: Enslow Publishers, 1995.

Hoag, Edwin, and Joy Hoag. *Masters of Modern Architecture: Frank Lloyd Wright, Le Corbusier, Mies van der Rohe, and Walter Gropius.* Indianapolis: Bobbs-Merrill, 1977.

Hubbard, Jan, ed. *The Official NBA Encyclopedia,* 2nd ed. New York: Doubleday, 2000.

Ingram, Philip. *Russia and the USSR: 1905–1991.* Cambridge, England: Cambridge University Press, 1997.

Judson, Karen. *The Presidency of the United States.* Springfield, NJ: Enslow Publishers, 1996.

Kallen, Stuart A., ed. *Nineteen Fifties.* San Diego: Greenhaven Press, 2000.

Katz, Ephraim. *The Film Encyclopedia,* 4th ed. New York: HarperResource, 2001.

Knapp, Ron. *American Legends of Rock.* Springfield, NJ: Enslow Publishers, 1996.

Kort, Michael. *China Under Communism.* Brookfield, CT: Millbrook Press, 1994.

Kort, Michael. *The Cold War.* Brookfield, CT: Millbrook Press, 1994.

Kort, Michael. *Russia.* New York: Facts on File, 1995.

Kroc, Ray, with Robert Anderson. *Grinding It Out: The Making of McDonald's.* Chicago: H. Regnery, 1977.

Krohn, Katherine E. *Marilyn Monroe: Norma Jean's Dream.* Minneapolis, MN: Lerner Publications, 1997.

Lampton, Christopher. *Wernher von Braun.* New York: Franklin Watts, 1988.

Larsen, Rebecca. *Oppenheimer and the Atomic Bomb.* New York: Franklin Watts, 1988.

Love, John F. *McDonald's: Behind the Arches.* New York: Bantam Books, 1986.

Lusane, Clarence. *No Easy Victories: Black Americans and the Vote.* New York: Franklin Watts, 1996.

Lusane, Clarence. *The Struggle for Equal Education.* New York: Franklin Watts, 1992.

Lynn, Elizabeth. *Babe Didrikson Zaharias.* New York: Chelsea House, 1989.

Macht, Norman L. *Roy Campanella: Baseball Star.* New York: Chelsea House, 1996.

Maltin, Leonard, ed. *Leonard Maltin's Movie Encyclopedia.* New York: Dutton, 1994.

Maltin, Leonard, ed. *Movie and Video Guide,* 22nd ed. New York: Signet, 2001.

Mays, Willie, with Lou Sahadi. *Say Hey: The Autobiography of Willie Mays.* New York: Simon & Schuster, 1988.

McCrohan, Donna. *The Honeymooners' Companion: The Kramdens and the Nortons Revisited.* New York: Workman Publishing Company, 1978.

McNeil, Alex. *Total Television,* 4th ed. New York: Penguin Books, 1996.

Monroe, Judy. *The Rosenberg Cold War Spy Trial: A Headline Court Case.* Berkeley Heights, NJ: Enslow Publishers, 2001.

Moss, Francis. *The Rosenberg Espionage Case.* San Diego: Lucent Books, 2000.

Nardo, Don. *Lasers: Humanity's Magic Light.* San Diego: Lucent Books, 1990.

Newton, David E. *James Watson and Francis Crick: Discovery of the Double Helix and Beyond.* New York: Facts on File, 1992.

Northrup, Mary. *American Computer Pioneers.* Springfield, NJ: Enslow Publishers, 1998.

O'Connell, Arthur J. *American Business in the 20th Century.* San Mateo, CA: Bluewood Books, 1999.

Oleksy, Walter. *The Importance of James Dean.* San Diego: Lucent Books, 2001.

Packard, Vance. *The Hidden Persuaders.* New York: McKay, 1957.

Parks, Rosa, with Jim Haskins. *My Story.* New York: Dial Books, 1992.

Rappaport, Doreen. *The Alger Hiss Trial.* New York: HarperCollins, 1993.

Rasmussen, R. Kent. *Farewell Jim Crow: The Rise and Fall of Segregation in America.* New York: Facts on File, 1997.

Ritter, Lawrence. *The Story of Baseball,* rev. ed. New York: Morrow Junior Books, 1999.

Rubin, Susan Goldman. *Frank Lloyd Wright.* New York: Harry N. Abrams, 1994.

Rummel, Jack. *Robert Oppenheimer: Dark Prince.* New York: Facts on File, 1992.

Schraff, Anne E. *Coretta Scott King: Striving for Civil Rights.* Springfield, NJ: Enslow Publishers, 1997.

Schrecker, Ellen. *The Age of McCarthyism.* Boston: Bedford Books of St. Martin's Press, 1994.

Schultz, Charles M. *Peanuts: A Golden Celebration.* New York: Harper Resource, 1999.

Schuman, Michael. *Martin Luther King, Jr.: Leader for Civil Rights.* Springfield, NJ: Enslow Publishers, 1996.

Scott, Robert A. *Douglas MacArthur and the Century of War.* New York, Facts on File, 1997.

Senker, Cath. *Rosalind Franklin.* Austin, TX: Raintree/Steck-Vaughn, 2002.

Sherrow, Victoria. *James Watson and Francis Crick: Decoding the Secrets of DNA.* Woodbridge, CT: Blackbirch Press, 1995.

Shirley, David. *The History of Rock & Roll.* New York: Franklin Watts, 1987.

Slocum, Frank. *Topps Baseball Cards: The Complete Picture Collection, a 40 Year History, 1951–1990.* New York, Warner Books, 1990.

Southard, Andy and Tony Thacker. *Custom Cars of the 1950s.* Osceola, WI: Motorbooks International, 1993.

Southard, Andy. *Hot Rods and the 1950s.* Osceola, WI: Motorbooks International, 1995.

Spangenburg, Ray, and Diane K. Moser. *Wernher von Braun: Space Visionary and Rocket Engineer.* New York: Facts on File, 1995.

Stewart, Mark. *Baseball: A History of the National Pastime.* New York: Franklin Watts, 1998.

Stewart, Mark. *Basketball: A History of Hoops.* New York: Franklin Watts, 1999.

Stewart, Mark. *Football: A History of the Gridiron Game.* New York: Franklin Watts, 1998.

Thorn, John, Pete Palmer, and Michael Gershman, eds. *Total Baseball,* Kingston, NY: Total Sports, 2001.

Thro, Ellen. *Robotics: The Marriage of Computers and Machines.* New York, Facts on File, 1993.

Topalian, Elyse. *Margaret Sanger.* New York: Franklin Watts, 1984.

Tushnet, Mark V. *Brown v. Board of Education: The Battle for Integration.* New York: Franklin Watts, 1996.

Vaughan, William H. T. *Encyclopedia of Artists.* New York: Oxford University Press, 2000.

Vernell, Marjorie. *Leaders of Black Civil Rights.* San Diego: Lucent Books, 2000.

Wakeman, Nancy. *Babe Didrikson Zaharias: Driven to Win.* Minneapolis, MN: Lerner Publications, 2000.

Weiss, Ann E. *Easy Credit.* Brookfield, CT: Twenty-First Century Books, 2000.

Wellman, Sam. *Billy Graham: The Great Evangelist.* Uhrichsville, OH: Barbour & Company, 1996.

Whitelaw, Nancy. *Margaret Sanger: Every Child a Wanted Child.* New York: Dillon Press, 1994.

Whitfield, Stephen J. *A Death in the Delta: The Story of Emmett Till.* New York: Free Press, 1988; Baltimore, Johns Hopkins University Press, 1991 (reprint).

Whittingham, Richard. *Rites of Autumn: The Story of College Football.* New York: Free Press, 2001.

Whyte Jr., William H. *The Organization Man.* New York: Simon & Schuster, 1956.

Willard, Charlotte. *Frank Lloyd Wright: American Architect.* New York: MacMillan, 1972.

Williams, Ted, with David Pietrusza. *Ted Williams: My Life in Pictures.* Kingston, NY: Total Sports, 2001.

Wilson, Camilla. *Rosa Parks: From the Back of the Bus to the Front of a Movement.* New York: Scholastic Paperbacks, 2001.

Winkler, Allan M. *The Cold War: A History in Documents.* New York: Oxford University Children's Books, 2001.

Wooten, Susan McIntosh. *Billy Graham: World-Famous Evangelist.* Berkeley Heights, NJ: Enslow Publishers, 2001.

Wormser, Richard. *The Rise & Fall of Jim Crow: The African-American Struggle Against Discrimination, 1865–1954.* New York: Franklin Watts, 1999.

WEB SITES

AFL-CIO Main Page. http://www.aflcio.org/home.htm (accessed on August 9, 2002).

Where to Learn More

....

American Experience/A Brilliant Madness. http://www.pbs.org/wgbh/amex/nash/timeline/timeline2.html (accessed on August 9, 2002).

The American 1950s. http://www.english.upenn.edu/~afilreis/50s/home.html (accessed on August 9, 2002).

Attachment Across Cultures—Research Report. http://www.attachmentacrosscultures.org/research/supplement.html (accessed on August 9, 2002).

Biographies: Louis Leakey. http://www.talkorigins.org/faqs/homs/lleakey.html (accessed on August 9, 2002).

Boxing on TV. http://www.skypoint.com/members/schutz19/boxing.htm (accessed on August 9, 2002).

A Brief History of Distance Education. http://www.seniornet.org/edu/art/history.html (accessed on August 9, 2002).

Fashion Flashbacks. http://www.fashion-flashbacks.com/20cen/20cen1950s.html (accessed on August 9, 2002).

Fear of Polio in the 1950s. http://www.inform.umd.edu/HONR/HONR269J/.WWW/projects/sokol.html (accessed on August 9, 2002).

The First Fifty Years of Business Computing Timeline. http://www.cioinsight.com/article2/0,3959,51554,00.asp (accessed on August 9, 2002).

From Plessy v. Ferguson to Brown v. Board of Education: the Supreme Court Rules on School Desegregation. http://www.yale.edu/ynhti/pubs/A5/wolff.html (accessed on August 9, 2002).

History of Space Exploration: Sputnik Satellite Program. http://www.nauts.com/vehicles/50s/sputnik.html (accessed on August 9, 2002).

Introduction to the Court Opinion on the Brown v. Board of Education Case. http://usinfo.state.gov/usa/infousa/facts/democrac/36.htm (accessed on August 9, 2002).

Legacy of McCarthyism. http://www.english.upenn.edu/~afilreis/50s/schrecker-legacy.html (accessed on August 9, 2002).

Major League Baseball Historical Standings 1950s. http://www.fortunecity.com/olympia/zatopek/91/1950s.html (accessed on August 9, 2002).

The 1950s. http://www.nikemissile.net/Coldwar/1950s.html (accessed on August 9, 2002).

The 1950s: Era of the Mass Disease Campaign. http://www.unicef.org/sowc96/1950s.htm (accessed on August 9, 2002).

1950s Timeline. http://www.cdc.gov/eis/about/timeline.htm (accessed on August 9, 2002).

Pop Art. http://www.artchive.com/artchive/pop_art.html (accessed on August 9, 2002).

Pro Football Hall of Fame—History. http://www.profootballhof.com/history/mainpage.cfm?cont_id=113955 (accessed on August 9, 2002).

Rebels: Painters and Poets of the 1950s. http://www.npg.si.edu/exh/rebels/poets.htm (accessed on August 9, 2002).

Sakharov's H-Bomb. http://www.thebulletin.org/issues/1990/o90/o90bethe.html (accessed on August 9, 2002).

Timeline, 1950. http://hammer.prohosting.com/~penz/computer/time1950.htm (accessed on August 9, 2002).

USAF Museum. http://www.wpafb.af.mil/museum/50th/event50.htm (accessed on August 9, 2002).

White House Historical Association—Timeline. http://www.whitehousehistory. org/04_history/subs_timeline/a_presidents/frame_a_1950.html (accessed on August 9, 2002).

Index